PROMISES ON

Velvet Wings

PROMISES ON

Velvet Wings

POEMS OF FAITH,

FAMILY, FRIENDS,

AND FUN

REGINA MCAFEE

XULON PRESS

Xulon Press
2301 Lucien Way #415
Maitland, FL 32751
407.339.4217
www.xulonpress.com

Paperback ISBN-13: 978-1-66286-768-2
Ebook ISBN-13: 978-1-66286-769-9

Dedication

This book is dedicated to my sweet husband who encouraged me throughout the process of putting this manuscript together. It is also dedicated to the family and friends who smiled, or better yet, laughed when I read a poem out loud. Maybe you hit "like" or made a nice comment when I shared a poem on Facebook.

This book is especially dedicated to friends who asked, "When are you going to publish a poetry book?" You were the catalyst that got me started on this project and the fuel that kept me going. How blessed I am to be able to share my love of life, and my love for my Lord and Savior Jesus Christ, through the poems in this book.

Foreword

There are many wonderful things to write about Mrs. Regina McAfee. I first met her in October 1991 when I began working as a classroom assistant in fourth grade at North Rock Creek School in Shawnee, OK. She and her aunt, Evelyn Anderson, were two fourth grade teachers. Mrs. McAfee loved her students and loved teaching. She retired after 32 years in education but missed teaching students. She came out of retirement and is teaching part time at a local public school.

Mrs. McAfee's poems are about the valuable things in her life. Her faith is the principal factor of which she interacts with areas in her life. There were countless times she and I joined hands and prayed to our Creator for family, students, and friends. She takes the utmost pride in providing love and care for her family. She and her husband, William, were high school sweethearts and have been married for over 56 years. Mrs. McAfee loves cooking and cleaning her house. She has publicly declared her love of shopping at Walmart. Sunday dinners after church are special gatherings for immediate and extended family. Community members have also eaten at the McAfee table. Wonderful, lasting memories are made when family and friends congregate at the McAfee home to talk, eat, and laugh together.

Mrs. McAfee loves to talk to everyone! An example of her love of people is a trip I invited her to take with me to Mexico. We had a five day stay touring the local sites. Once, we boarded a tour van with eight people. We knew no one on that van except ourselves. It did not take long for Mrs. McAfee to introduce herself to the person next to her. That started the other people talking with each other. Very soon we knew the names and hometowns of each of the riders. On another tour van to a site, Mrs.

McAfee talked with a young couple from England. Had it not been for her outgoing personality, we would not have two new Facebook friends.

Mrs. McAfee loves to have fun! She's not afraid to laugh at herself. One school day, she was reviewing spelling words with students. The word was "mesa" (may-suh). She pronounced it mess-uh. After she learned the correct pronunciation of the word, she said, "I made a mess-uh out of that one!" There are many occasions which produced a lot of laughter between us and her numerous friends. During a school day, friendly joking was going on between us. I left my classroom to make copies in the workroom. After returning to my room, I sat at my desk, and there she was hiding under my desk!

School colleagues looked forward to one of "Regina's poems" when they retired from teaching. She gifted each retiree with a special poem. The poem she wrote for my retirement was 30 years in the making. Mrs. McAfee has written an abundance of poems of her faith, family, friends, and fun. You are in for a very special treat as you read these poems. Relax in your favorite chair as you enjoy this masterpiece.

Esther Bell
October, 2022

Preface

When I was a young girl, I dug a hole in the side of a canyon and hid a cigar box containing notebook paper and pencils. That's where I learned it was a joy to put my thoughts down on paper. I would slip away from the house, meander through the woods to my secret place, and spend time writing poems and stories. Before I headed back to the house, I would hide that cigar box containing the treasured writings by covering the opening of the little cave with leaves and sticks. Those first writings were "for my eyes" only. (Though I may have occasionally read a story to a feathered friend or a feisty squirrel.)

The first poem I remember writing contained the words, "She has eyes of blue; the kind of eyes that say, 'I love you.'" I wrote that poem for my precious Aunt Laveda Dockrey. She beamed with such joy when I read that poem to her. She made a ten year old girl feel very special. I think that's when I quit hiding the writings in the cigar box.

It was a wonderful time growing up in the 1950's surrounded by extended family and kind neighbors. There were three churches in the community and each of the churches had a positive influence on my life. I heard about Jesus in Sunday School at the Johnson Church of God. When we sang the song "Jesus Loves Me", I knew that He loved me!

The first time I remember talking to Jesus was on a walk through the woods to my grandmother's house. I had a very vivid imagination and I just knew there was a panther following me. I reached my hand up to the sky and said, "Jesus, I'm afraid, take my hand." There was a peace that flooded my heart and all the fear was gone. Jesus did take my hand and he has walked with me all the years of my life.

Besides the churches in the community, there was a little country store and a small two room school (Johnson Grade School.) I enjoyed school so much and I loved my 1st-4th grade teacher, Mrs. Cheek. Her husband, Mr. Cheek taught 5th-8th grade.

It was at this little country school that I discovered the joy of sharing friendship with other children my age and the joy of reading and writing. I decided I wanted to be a teacher in second grade while listening to Mrs. Cheek read to the class. There were box suppers, Christmas plays, and playing on a basketball team. The setting for the poem "The Nickel Lemon" was from that little school.

Treasured memories from my childhood have been the theme for many of the poems. I have written several poems of faith. My faith in Jesus is the foundation of who I am. Jesus has walked with me through difficult times and joyful times. The words, "I will never leave you or forsake you," or the words, "I can do all things through Christ who gives me strength," along with other scriptures, have kept me going and given me joy and purpose.

When I have felt overwhelmed or worried about some of the challenges of life, Jesus has always shown me His faithfulness. Sometimes He speaks to me through the beauty of a sunrise, the singing of the birds, colorful wildflowers, or a butterfly sipping nectar from a flower. I named this book "Promises on Velvet Wings," because I have witnessed how He takes care of His delicate creations by always providing what they need, and He always provides what we need.

About 15 years ago my dad passed away and my husband and I, along with three of our sons, moved into the house that I helped my daddy build when I was five. There are so many memories from growing up in this house. This house is surrounded by the woods where my brothers and sister and I played. Through those woods is the place where I would hide the writings of the "little girl me" in a cigar box. I still attend the church where I first learned about Jesus. The three churches are still shining the light of Jesus in the community.

I pray this book will bring a smile to someone's face and encourage someone by reminding the reader just how precious they are to the Lord. I pray that His light shines through these poems. Always remember the formula for J.O.Y. is Jesus, Others, and You.

In that order. Always.

Acknowledgements

A special thank you to my family for showing such excitement when I shared the idea of publishing a poetry book. Thank you to my granddaughter, Emily Pryor, who helped me get the poems in order on the computer.

Thank you to a dear friend from church, Crystal Snyder, whose patience and photographic skills captured the perfect picture for the cover of this book.

Thank you to my husband who listened to me read each poem numerous times and never seemed to get tired of hearing them and almost always commented, "That's a good one!"

Thank you to my dear friend, Esther Bell, who wrote the "Foreword" for this book. I wrote many poems for friends who were retiring over the many years I worked at North Rock Creek School. The poem for Mrs. Bell was the last "retirement poem" I wrote. It was such a joy reading it at her retirement reception.

I could not have put this book together without the help of a friend and coworker at Earlsboro School, Carra Crow, who helped me with computer questions and allowed me to spend many hours at her computer. An eighth grade student, Bailey Nadeau, also gave me valuable input and encouraged me through the process. I would also like to acknowledge the current Earlsboro seventh grade reading class who helped write the poem, "Onomatopoeia" in the spring of 2022.

Finally, I want to thank my Heavenly Father for the help He has given me in writing these poems. Sometimes He would wake me in the middle of the night and I could barely keep up with the pen as He gave me the words to write. Sometimes, I would get an idea for a poem, or a friend would ask me to write a poem, and it would be a bit of a struggle. But, as I prayed and asked for His guidance, He always answered my prayer.

Table of Contents

Faith

Promises on Velvet Wings

The road curved next to a field of green;
My destination in sight—then this scene:
Little pink flowers that barely caught my eye,
With delicate little petals open to the sky.

Sipping the flower's nectar was a pretty thing,
A beautiful butterfly with delicate wings,
Black wings, trimmed in rich metallic blue,
"Hello pretty thing; may I watch you?"

My presence was of no concern at all,
As Mr. Velvet drank from a cup so small.
I thought, as I watched his fluttering wings,
Set before him is a banquet fit for kings.

He flutters from petal to petal with no care;
God's provided him with nectar everywhere!
Consider the lilies, the sparrow, the butterfly;
I felt His nearness as I looked to the blue sky.

I continued on—my destination in sight,
My purpose, my faith, my joy at a new height;
As I remembered, "God is in control of all things."
A promise delivered on velvet wings.

Lessons for Life

We have a loving Father;
    His presence is always near.
He has promised He will never
    leave you; give Him your fear.

We have a loving Father;
    He guides us down life's road.
His all powerful arms are open;
    give Him your load.

We have a loving Father;
    to the world He is a stranger.
Keep your heart pure and full
    of love; give Him your anger.

We have a loving Father;
    His Son bore our sin and strife.
He wants to be in fellowship
    with you; give Him your life!

Learning about Jesus

In a little country church,
    many years ago,
I learned about Jesus and
    . that He loves me so.
The preacher opened the Bible
    and I knew It was God's word;
Even as a child, my heart was stirred
    by the message I heard.

I heard about a miraculous birth
    of a baby born in a stable;
I heard about miracles–He was the
    Son of God And He was able:
To feed 5000 with two fish and
    five small loaves of bread,
To calm the raging storm, heal the sick,
    and even raise the dead.

I heard about His love for me
    and that he died for my sin;
I felt His presence and I joyfully
    gave my heart to Him.
I learned, as the years passed,
    that His Word is completely true;
I've especially held to the verse that says,
    "I will never leave you."

I heard the story of the disciples' joy at
    discovering the empty tomb.
That my Savior ascended to Heaven
    where He is preparing me a room.

I remember the joy as we sang,
    "Jesus loves me this I know."
A joy discovered in a little country church
    many years ago.

The Birds and I Sing for Joy

The full moon shines brightly through
    the branches of the magnolia tree,
While the birds sing their lovely "Good
    Morning" songs so joyfully.

I woke up early—4:00 or so—with just
    a few worries on my mind;
I do that sometimes even though I would
    say I'm not the worryin' kind.
Then, I remembered, before the worries
    lasted very long,
About who I am in Jesus and I remembered
    the words to a song:

"Let us have a little talk with Jesus…"

So, I just opened up my heart to praise
    Him and I began to sing;
Those worries vanished! The joy of the
    Lord is a wonderful thing.
Time and time again our Savior has
    answered our prayers;
He is with us each step of the way and
    for each of us He truly cares.

Goodbye worries; the Lord has given
    me the gift of a brand new day.
I seek His guidance on what to do, where
    to go, and the words to say.
The full moon shines brightly through
    the branches of the Magnolia tree,
While the birds and I sing our "Good
    Morning," songs so very joyfully.

Philippians 4:6, 7

Do not be anxious about anything, but in everything, by prayer and petition, with thanksgiving, present your requests to God. And the peace of God, which transcends all understanding, will guard your hearts and your minds in Christ Jesus.

The Fruit of the Spirit
(Galatians 5; 22-23)

Love: May the redemptive Love of Jesus
    completely fill our hearts today;
The Love that spurs us to take action to serve
    others in an unselfish way.

Joy: A deep refreshing spring bubbling
    from a heart that does not hate;
A heart so in tune with Him that yearnings
    deep within say, "Trust and Wait".

Peace: Without Love and Joy, you cannot exist,
    for it is in them you are born;
For hate, bitterness, and anger drive nails
    into the heart that is bitter and torn.

Patience: You show up in long lines and red lights
    and times that say, "Wait!"
You smile at the shenanigans of impish children;
    you choose not to berate!

Goodness: A hand extended, in love, to a hurting
    world in need of His Grace;
Small acts of selflessness that warm the heart
    and put a smile on your face.

Kindness: You are the twin of goodness,
    and we should share you everywhere;
You are a smile, a warm greeting, a gentle reminder
    that says to others, "I care".

Faithfulness: Here is the solid foundation
    on which we steadfastly take a stand;
Through chaos, uncertainty, change, and adversity,
    we never let go of His hand.

Gentleness: He is gentle with us—no cruel,
    rough fingers tearing us apart;
Through His word and prayer comes the strength
    of a gentle, caring heart.

Self Control: To do, say, and think what is wise
    and prudent is hard to do;
The war between the flesh and spirit is real,
    but God will strengthen you.

To bear this Fruit so graciously given, we must stay
    firmly grafted in the Vine;
We, the branches, empowered by the One who declares,
    "Child, you are mine!"

Embrace Faith

Embrace faith; gather up and give
    your fears to your Father above;
Despite the bleak circumstances,
    we can trust His unfailing love.

We simply cannot see the entire picture
    through our human eyes;
We can trust our Heavenly Father–
    to Him this is not a surprise.

We were created for something
    far beyond this time on Earth,
Destined to be a part of a Divine plan
    even before our birth.

There's something going on far beyond
    our ability to comprehend;
Take rest and comfort knowing our Creator
    knows how this will end.

I'm going to trust Him who has promised
    to never leave nor forsake me;
I know I am going to spend my life loving
    Him from now and through eternity.

When it seems it's too much–
    the task is too demanding;
He will fortify you with strength
    and peace beyond understanding.

In our weakness, we become strong
    when we cling to our Father above;
Despite the bleak circumstances we can
    always trust in His unfailing love.

    Embrace Faith!

Night Patrol

Look!
Look at the myrtle trees.
Those dark shapes are not shadows,
But great steeds!

Mounted by Angels who ride at night.
The red one, the sorrel, and the white.
Look! Can you see them? What a sight!

In the Unseen World, they are there—
Often summoned by a prayer.
On patrol, they ride everywhere.

Look!
Look at the myrtle trees.
Those dark shapes are not shadows,
But great steeds!

Zechariah 1: 8-10

During the night I had a vision, and there before me was a man mounted on a red horse. He was standing among the myrtle trees in a ravine. Behind him were red, brown, and white horses.

I asked, "What are these, my Lord?"

The angel who was talking with me answered, "I will show you what they are."

Then the man standing among the myrtle tree explained, "They are the ones the Lord has sent to go throughout the earth."

Sunday School Prayer

Bless the little feet that walk through the door;
Some may have never been here before.
Help them feel as if they belong here;
Take away their doubts and fears.

Bless the little eyes that look around;
Seeing the things that might be found.
Bless the little hands as they work and play;
Help me let them make things their way.

Bless those who squeal and giggle,
And bless those who squirm and wiggle.
Bless those that are really shy,
And those who can't help but cry.

Help me your precious word to impart,
To each and every sweet tender heart.
Help me see them through your eyes,
Remembering they are so little in size.

Yes, Lord, bless the little hearts, hands, eyes, and feet,
Of these little lambs—the tiniest of your sheep!

Written in 1994 when I was teaching a preschool Sunday School class at the Johnson Church of God.

The Most Important Thing

It's early morning; time to get up.
Make the bed—hurry up!
Didn't get my papers graded last night;
Did I brush my hair? Do I look a fright?
Sure glad we got the bills in the mail;
Seems we don't manage money very well.
Life's worries weighin' heavier and heavier;
Then I remembered what's most important,
    and whispered a "Thank you" prayer.

Grab my school bag—head out the door;
Left my sack lunch sittin' on the kitchen floor!
Wishin' I hadn't had that fight
With my daughter last night.
Steps are gettin' lighter; day's lookin' brighter,
Greet each boy and girl with a smile;
So thankful I can be in this classroom for a while.

The day rushes by; we've had such fun.
Never enough time to get everything done.
Called my daughter, "I'm sorry about last night.
The things I said were not right."
Forgiveness is a precious gift,
That gives the heart a lift.
Life goes on with its ups and downs;
Sometimes a smile—sometimes a frown.

No matter what, each and every day,
Be thankful for Salvation and
Take time to pray.
"Thank you, Jesus, for Calvary's Way,
The blood you shed, my sins you bore,

I'm free from sin; in bondage no more!"
Thank you, Jesus, for this...
The most important thing!

I'M SAVED!

Remember

Father,

Let all who see this special tree

Remember

Remember the precious lives of men, women,
and children whose life on this earth has ended.

Remember those who have known a loss so great,
their broken hearts won't soon be mended.

Let all who see this special tree

Remember the outpouring of generosity and
love of our Great Nation and our State.

And remember the law of love is always greater
and more powerful than any act of hate.

Let all who see this special tree

Remember

Amen

*A dogwood tree was planted at North Rock Creek School on June 1,
1995, in memory of the victims of the April 19th bombing of the Murray
Federal Building in Oklahoma City. The symbol of the dogwood tree
is to remember events that profoundly affected history, and so is the
purpose of this poem.*

Little Country Church

In a little white country church,
    just down the road, several years ago,
The preacher told folks about Jesus;
    he wanted them to know...

He wanted them to know about love,
    and hope, and His amazing grace,
That even in the trials and sorrows of life,
    you can still run a joyful race.

I wonder if he ever grew discouraged;
    he worked another job as well.
He loved his lovely wife, the church pianist;
    the congregation could tell.

He and his wife had three pretty daughters
    and a handsome little son;
Those little country kids loved their parents
    and they knew how to have fun.

Years have passed and that precious voice
    is quiet, but the message goes on;
The good news of Jesus is being shared
    by his grandchildren–now grown.

The message of Jesus shared in a little
    country church, many years ago,
Continues on in Kenya, Africa, because
    those grandkids want the world to know!

*Dedicated to Pastor Ray Branson's family who continue to share the love
of Jesus with a hurting world. Bro. Branson's granddaughters, Sara and
Cara Branson, have served as missionaries in Kenya, Africa, for many
years. (Small churches can reach millions of people.)*

The Pastor Gardener

A gardener looks to books for information;
　　Our pastor looks to the Book of books.
A gardener plants seeds.
　　Our pastor plants the seeds of the Word.

When a gardener plants a seed, he has faith
　　the seed will produce fruit.
Our pastor believes the seeds of the Gospel
　　will produce fruit.

A gardener prays for rain.
　　Our pastor prays for spiritual rain.

A gardener wants the plants to grow
　　a good root system.
Our pastor prays his congregation will
　　be rooted in God's Word.

A gardener feels protective of the
　　tender new plants.
Our pastor feels protective of the tender
　　hearts of new Christians.

The gardener tends the plants
　　with love and care.
Our pastor tends his garden
　　with love and prayer.

A gardener watches for storms.
　　Our pastor does too.
A gardener gets up early.
　　So does our pastor.

A gardener produces a crop to share
    with a hungry world.
Our pastor prays his garden will share
    the love of Christ with the world.

Thank you, Heavenly Father,
    for Pastors everywhere,
Who lovingly tend the gardens
    you have put in their care.

You'd Fit Just Fine

If you don't attend church,
    you might want to consider it.
There's a pew, or a chair, and
    you'd fit just fine sitting in it.

There are songs to be sung: old, slow hymns,
    or new songs, loud and fast;
Songs that remind us there's One who never
    forsakes; His love always lasts.

There's the Word to be heard;
    it gives us strength to live life.
You might just hear the perfect scripture
    to deal with your strife.

You might make a commitment
    that would change your direction;
You might realize you're still walking
    around because of His protection.

If you don't attend church,
    you might want to consider it.
There's a pew or a chair somewhere
    and you'd fit just fine in it!

The Ladies' Meeting

In a little country church, there are smiles,
    warm hugs, and hearts greeting;
On a Saturday morning as we gathered
    for "The Ladies' Meeting".

There was plenty of good food and a fun game:
    "Bragging Rights" the prize.
There was a lot accomplished even though
    our number was small in size.

How can we help a hurting world;
    what would Jesus have us do?
We decided on a service project
    and prayed for special needs too.

A precious lady shared a devotion
    from Jeremiah 29:11;
He has a wonderful plan for all of us–
    our Father in Heaven.

Friends, come join us next time;
    there's plenty of seating.
We would love to fellowship with you
    at the "The Ladies' Meeting".

Happy Mother's Day

Happy Mother's Day to all you
    precious mommies;
To the young ones, the old ones,
    and all those in between.
To the new ones, the worn out ones,
    the sad ones—on God you lean!
To those who have shared your little
    ones, though your heart breaks;
Crazy circumstances, but you smile—
    no one sees how your heart aches.

It's wonderful to be a mommy, and
    it's challenging, but oh so fun.
It's sleepless nights and tears, and joy and
    laughter, with each precious little one.
It's sweet memories, and regrets, and loneliness
    that comes from an "empty nest".
It's hopefulness they'll make it without you,
    and that they know you did your best.
It's love—maybe the closest thing on earth
    to God's love—love like no other;
Daddies feel this depth of love also, and
    some daddies fill the role of mother.

To all you precious mommies,
    from my heart I say:
You are a treasure on earth dear ones;
    Happy Mother's Day!

The Good Samaritan's Wife

I wonder what the "Good Samaritan"
    faced when he got home.
Was it, "Where have you been? Why
    have you been gone so long?"

"Your boss has been looking for you—
    said you never came to work!
Said you need to be more responsible,
    your duties not to shirk!"

"What? What did you say? You helped
    a stranger along the way?
You gave him money and
    put him up in a motel?
Well now, that's just swell!"

"Me and the kids never
    get a vacation,
And you help some vagabond who got
    himself in a rough situation?"

"Well, did you at least make it home
    with the oil and wine?
It's half gone!
    Well now, that's just fine!"

"I'm having the neighbors over
    and we will probably run out!
You are such a selfish man;
    you spoil everything I plan!"

"I'm the laughing stock of Samaria
    putting up with you.
Go on, take care of the world.
    but, as for me, I'm through!"

Attitude has so much to do with
    what we face in life.
Maybe this was the response
    he received from his wife:

"Hi, Honey, where have you been?
    Seems you're a little late again.
What? You helped a man who had been
    beaten and robbed today?"

"I am so proud of the way
    you consider those in need.
There are so many people
    you have helped clothe and feed."

"I am so glad you have such
    a compassionate heart.
You know that's why I fell in love
    with you from the start."

"You gave the man some money?
    Well, that's wonderful honey.
You know every time we help
    someone in need,
God knows all about it and
    He blesses us indeed!"

"You are such a remarkably
    wonderful man;
I know marrying you was a part
    of His wonderful plan."

"I support you
    in all that you do,
And, Honey, have I told you lately
    I love you!"

He is Near

Soft and gentle start to the day filled
    with a sunrise of subtle hues,
As God comforts the fragile hearts
    that have been bruised.

Remember, Heaven has received those
    who have stepped away;
There is a promise—cling to that promise—
    you will be reunited one day.

Breathe deeply, step easily; use a soft voice
    and a gentle touch.
Be kind to yourself; your Heavenly Father
    loves you so much.

His healing hand is upon you;
    His presence removes every fear.
He whispers with gentle colors
    and the calm assurance He is near.

The Empty Space

"It's just not right," some people said,
"To have a Cross on the City Seal.
We must put something there instead,
Something which to all people will appeal."

And so in the heart of this little state,
There arose this most emotional debate.

"You don't understand," some would try to explain,
"What the Cross means, the message it proclaims.
To remove it is to attack our Christian foundation,
And the very heritage of our Christian Nation."

"In the Constitution it's plainly stated
That people's rights must not be violated;
There must be a separation of Church and State,"
And so continues this age old debate.

Now the Cross is removed and in its place
There is instead "An Empty Space!"

"It's just not right." some people said,
"For this man to talk of God's will.
He's got crazy ideas in his head;
His teachings to us do not appeal!"

And so the destiny of one man's fate
Would result in this most emotional debate.

"He doesn't understand," some tried to explain,
"How serious it is; the Temple he even defames.
If we don't get rid of him, he will destroy our Nation;
Crucify Him! The cross must be his destination!"

But, in God's Word His destiny was plainly stated,
That He would be mocked and by all men hated,
And placed in a tomb outside the city gate—
All a part of God's plan to destroy death and hate.

And just as God planned, He rose from that place;
And in that tomb He left "An Empty Space!"

"Your heart is not right," the Spirit said,
"You're missing God's purpose and will.
You're controlled by selfish motives instead,"
With great conviction the Holy Spirit did appeal.

And in my heart's sinful state
There arose this most emotional debate.

"You need to understand," God's word would explain,
"What the Cross means—the message it proclaims.
It's the answer to your life's foundation;
It's the price Jesus paid for your salvation."

"And in My Word it is plainly stated
That the laws of righteousness You violated.
Believe on Jesus and be separated from sin's state;
For He settled sin's debt—there is no room for debate!

And the message of the Cross has filled the place
Where my heart used to have "An Empty Space!"

On the official Seal of the City of Edmond there
Is an empty space where the Cross used to be;
Let that empty space be a reminder of the empty tomb,
And how Jesus died on the Cross for you and for me.

The Sacred Cross...
    Nothing could ever take its place!
I will always remember the Cross
    when I see "The Empty Space!"

The Cross was removed from the City Seal in Edmond, Oklahoma, in 1996. The city council voted to leave an empty space where the Cross had been. I wrote this poem in 1996.

A Pastor's Prayer

Father, you've given me a garden to tend,
    a precious garden–the souls of men.
There are precious women and children too,
    and God, they all have a need for You.

Sometimes weeds try to creep in this garden:
    weeds of worry, gloom, and despair.
Help me, Father, to keep the weeds out of this
    garden you have put in my care.

Help me sow the seed of your word, and
    help others to share what they've heard.
The world needs to know of your love and care;
    there are hurting people everywhere.

Sometimes, Father, the garden seems
    more than I can tend.
My heart grows weary when I see the hurts
    of little children, women, and men.

Sometimes it seems there's just
    too much to do.
Then I remember the garden and the
    gardener are refreshed by you.

Thank you, Father, for the garden
    you have put in my care.
Help this garden produce fruit
    and to a hungry world to share.

Early Morning Prayer

In the early morning hours
    before the sun had risen,
I prayed for you.

I prayed that God would increase
    your strength and wisdom, and
I thanked God for you.

I asked God to increase the joy in
    all your days and I smiled as
I thought about you.

You added joy to my morning
    as I prayed for you,
In the early morning hours
    before the sun had risen.

He Named the Stars

He named the 3,000 stars
 we see on a moonless night.
He named the 100,000 you see
 when you hold a telescope just right.

He named the 100 billion stars
 in the Milky Way Galaxy.
There are billions of galaxies
 not yet revealed to you and me.

And He named their stars;
 He named them all!
The God we serve is mighty;
 don't you make Him small!

He named the stars and He knows
 the names of each of us.
His love is as infinite as the stars,
 and in His love I will trust!

Psalms 147:4
He counts the number of the stars; He calls them by name.

All is Well

I want to be an "All is well" kind of person,
Rising above circumstances, frustration, and fears.
I want to be an "All is well" kind of person,
Reflecting His love in my life through my years.

I want to be an "All is well" kind of person,
Whose heart stays focused on His purpose in my life,
An "All is well" kind of person who realizes:
There is an answer for life's craziness, chaos, and strife.

I want to be an "All is well" kind of person
Reflecting the light of Jesus to hurting humanity;
Not a "Woe is me" kind of person, wringing
My hands in despair and grasping at my sanity.

I want to be an "All is well" kind of person
Strengthened and empowered by His word;
Sharing the hope, joy, peace, kindness, and love
Of a Savior to a world who has not heard.

I want to be an "All is well" kind of person!

The story of "Elisha and the Shunamite Woman" inspired this poem. (2 Kings 4:8-37)

Cling to His Promises

There are two distinct narratives on
    the T.V. and Social Media;
(Don't try to prove you have all the
    answers from Wikipedia.)

"Four more years of that man and our
    Country is doomed," some say.
Others, equally concerned, "Vote for him,
    and lose the American Way."

Is the Media leaning to "The Left" as
    many folks seem to muse?
Are the stories shared by some on the
    "Right" only serving to confuse?

Are people really being shot in the streets
    because of the hat they wear?
Is it really peaceful protests, or acts
    of violence to dominate and scare?

Most of us can agree, regardless of our
    political affiliation,
To love and serve our neighbor is what
    makes this a great Nation.

I will not live in fear or dread as
    this crazy election draws near;
I will ask my Heavenly Father how
    I can serve others while I am here.

I will share what has been given to me;
    I have more than I need.
I will love my neighbor as myself, and
    to his Word I will heed.

I will love you no matter who you vote
    for and I will respect your view;
I'll cling to His promises as I remember
    the love He has for me and you.

August 31, 2020.

An Invisible Hand

An invisible hand pushes on my chest
    making it hard to breathe.
I will stay in this bed; let others take over,
    I'm too tired to leave.

Grab them…read them…they are a
    powerhouse of strength.
Scriptures—God's unfailing promises—
    long or short, any length.

Hidden in my heart, there on the
    Bible App, and in The Book,
I whisper a prayer and search the Word.
    (It is to Him I always look.)

An invisible hand takes mine and lifts
    me from the miry clay.
"I can do all things in Christ Jesus,"
    I am out of bed and on my way!

Dance Daughter Dance

Come to me my child;
Come give me a chance.
Come my precious daughter;
Come and join the dance!

I gave my life for you;
My love compares to none.
I want your heart to dance with me;
I want to waltz with you my precious one!

I do not condemn you;
Come, and hear my song.
Believe on me my precious child;
I'll cleanse you from all wrong.

Come, let me hold you close;
I want to dance with you—today and tomorrow.
I want you to know you are never alone;
Let me wipe away your tears of sorrow.

You, my love, my beautiful one,
My precious treasure;
You can't imagine the love I have for you,
A love without measure.

Look in my eyes;
You will only see Love.
Listen to the melody;
Miraculous music from above.

Come to me, my child;
Come, give me a chance.
Come, my precious daughter;
Come and join the dance.

He Hears Your Tears

When you try to pray but as hard as you try
All you can do is fold your weary hands and cry,
He hears your tears.

When, during sleepless nights, you seek relief,
But, you seem to be smothering in cold dark grief,
He hears your tears.

When you wonder if things will ever be right;
You seem to be struggling both day and night,
He hears your tears.

Just rest in His arms; your tears are enough;
Nothing needs to be said when life is so rough,
He hears your tears.

He will restore your joy; He will calm your fears.
Rest gentle heart, hang on; He hears your tears.
He hears your tears.

I Knelt at the Manger

I knelt at the manger and held the
little baby close to me;
Somehow the heavens parted and
Love was all I could see.
The love of God was placed in
a manger that day;
"I love you sweet Baby Jesus,"
was all I could say.

I knelt at the cross where fresh blood
dripped on the ground.
My heart was broken but I felt
such love all around.
The love of God hung on the
cross that day.
"I love you sweet Jesus,"
was all I could say.

I helped anoint his fragile body,
tears streaming down my face;
With heavy hearts we carried him
to his burial place.
I knelt at the tomb, my heart
broken on that bitter day.
"I love you, my dear friend, Jesus,"
I said, as I walked away.

With heart pounding, I ran from the
empty tomb; how could this be?
"He is not there, he is risen–he is alive!"
I proclaimed joyfully.
I knelt at his nail scarred feet, and with
tears, I looked at his love filled face;
"I love you, my dear precious Savior, thank
you for your Amazing Grace."

I knelt at the manger, held the little baby
close to me;
Somehow the heavens parted, and
Love was all I could see.

That Old Robber: Worry

It is so easy to get entangled with that
　　Old Robber: Worry!

　　He robs you of Peace and Joy.
　　He robs you of laughter.
　　He robs you of energy.
　　He robs you of sleep.

Sometimes, he ties you up with a strong
rope of anger and frustration.

He causes you to say things you wish you
hadn't said.

Lock that ole thief out of your heart by
using the powerful weapon of God's Word.

God's children should not be bound by that
Old Robber: Worry!

Philippians 4: 6-7

*Do not be anxious about anything, but in every situation, by prayer
and petition, with thanksgiving, present your requests to God and the
peace of God, which passes all understanding shall keep your hearts and
minds through Christ Jesus.*

Sometimes

Sometimes dark shadows fall around us
and the going gets tough.
There is conflict in families, sorrows
abound with troubles enough.

Sometimes disturbing questions choke our
reasoning as we wonder, "Why?"
With shaking hands and knots in our
stomachs, we crumble; we cry.

Mental illness, misunderstandings,
confusion, and grief.
Only through the strength of unwavering
faith can we find relief.

Life is beautiful, days are pleasant,
families embrace each other in love;
Fathers walk their daughters down the
aisle as the Angels smile from above.

Babies are born and cuddled in the arms
of new mommies with joy;
Daddies look on in gladness of heart
whether it be a girl or a boy.

Doors are opened when there didn't seem
there would ever be a way;
Hope lightens loads and elevates the heart
to anticipate a beautiful new day.

Sometimes!

A Warrior Went Home

A warrior went home; I learned
    that just a few days ago,
When the pastor shared the news
    about Brother Crow.

This precious man came to church
    when he was able,
And listened as the pastor fed us
    at our spiritual table.

This kind gentleman seemed
    to become increasingly more frail,
After his dear wife went to Heaven,
    he missed her so; we could tell.

Brother Crow went to the front
    of the church for prayer one Sunday;
"You see a man, frail and walking slowly,"
    I felt the Lord say;

"But I see a Warrior!"

"He has fought battles in prayer
    that have changed the course of history.
He has summoned Angels to protect
    his children; this is no mystery."

"He is a warrior dressed for battle
    with his armament in place;
I will strengthen this warrior
    until he finishes his race."

After that Sunday, I never saw
  Brother Crow the same as before.
I knew a strong man full of God's
  power had come through the door.

I saw a Warrior!

Now, that warrior, that precious man
  has gone home to join his wife,
To see his precious Savior whom he served
  with joy as he lived his life.

We who remain must take up the slack
  and pray a little more each day;
We must straighten our helmets, tighten
  our belts, and show others the way.

Brother Crow has fought his last battle;
  he was surely one of the best.
The Lord has said, "Welcome home,
  Soldier, it's time to rest!"

"Welcome Home Warrior!"

Ephesians 10:14-17
Stand firm then, with the belt of truth buckled around your waist
and with your feet fitted with the readiness that comes from the gospel
of peace.

In addition to all of this, take the shield of faith, with which you can
extinguish all the flaming arrows of the evil one. Take the helmet of
salvation and the sword of the Spirit which is the word of God.

Seeing Jesus

There was a time many years ago when I had
    such a longing to see my Savior's face;
I would imagine that I was looking in his
    kind eyes and giving him a warm embrace.

I wanted to see him; I had heard accounts of
    people who had seen our Savior so dear.
"Jesus," I would pray, "I know I will see you
    in Heaven, but I want to see you here."

That longing stayed in my heart for many
    a night and many a day,
Then my precious Savior whispered to my
    heart and I heard him say,

"I want you to see me in that homeless man
    in the park needing a meal;
I want you to see me in the eyes of a hurting
    world and understand how they feel."

"I want you to see me in the little ones looking
    for a place to call home;
I want you to see me in the stranger on the
    street who feels lost and alone."

"You won't have to look very far," my sweet
    Jesus said, "I am everywhere!
I am revealing myself to you in the way I
    choose; you show the world I care."

Birthday Blessings

As I straighten the house
    on this birthday morn,
I think about the many blessings
    I've had since I was born.

As I dust the many trinkets
    given to me with love,
I whisper a prayer of thanks
    to my Heavenly Father above.

I think about the many dreams
    I had as a little girl—
That was a long time ago, but
    the time passed in a whirl.

I married my childhood sweetheart
    and he's "still the one";
We've raised five beautiful daughters
    and a handsome son.

We have seven grandchildren—
    that's something to treasure;
The joy they have brought to us
    is really beyond measure.

My "little girl dream" of becoming
    a teacher came true;
And the dream of going
    on a mission trip did too.

I always dreamed of having
    a house full of girls and boys;
The fulfillment of that dream
    is one of my greatest joys!

I pray I have many more birthdays–
    I'm having so much fun;
Life's very interesting with
    three little boys–I love each one!

I treasure my faith, my family,
    and each precious friend;
When I start counting blessings,
    there seems to be no end.

Thank you, Lord, for the parents
    you gave me when I was born,
And thank you for the joy I feel
    on this wonderful birthday morn!

Written on my 58th birthday, February 23, 2008.

Wake up Dreams

Sometimes I find myself drifting back
    to simpler times,
When life seemed easier and my heart
    was full of rhymes.

Sometimes I think about the way
    things used to be,
When I giggled with four little girls—
    a happy young mommy.

Sometimes I ponder too much
    about choices I've made,
And I wonder if the choices
    were worth the trade.

My days have been precious
    as a teacher, a mommy, and a wife;
Sometimes I wonder if I deserved
    such a blessed life.

A preacher caught my attention
    and made me ponder;
Are there still dreams alive?
    Or just memories? Made me wonder…

Wake up dreams! They're in there—
    in this heart filled with busy days;
I'll treasure the memories, but there
    are dreams to awaken in the haze.

Wake up dreams!

A Precious Treasure

I have a treasure in my heart,
    a treasure worth more than gold,
A treasure that has sustained me
    more than could ever be told.

This treasure is God's Word
    planted deep in my heart,
That includes Bible stories of courage
    and wisdom for a start.

Bible stories of purpose and direction
    to travel through life.
Bible verses to calm and encourage
    in times of strife.

My mother and daddy are singing
    in treasured memories, "Look!
They are joyfully singing hymns
    from the old red song book!"

Mother, smiling and praising God
    before she left for Glory.
Daddy saying, "Keep your faith strong."
    (That's a part of his story!)

My heart beats in rhythm with
    the treasure of old time praise,
In a little country church from my young
    to my "not so young" days.

Thank you to all who helped
    plant the seeds of faith divine;
I pray that everyone would have
    a precious treasure like mine.

Did She Know?

Did she know as she knelt by the make-shift crib,
    that her little baby would bear such a load?
Did she know as she looked at his tiny feet,
    that they would walk Golgotha's road?

Did she know as she heard the lamb's soft bleat,
    mixed with her baby's cry,
Did she know He would shed his blood and
    no more little lambs would have to die?

Did she know as she looked at the tiny hand cradled
    in Joseph's roughened one,
Did she know that someday spikes would be driven
    into the hands of her precious son?

Did she know as she caressed his soft little cheeks
    and kissed his little head,
Did she know a kiss would betray him and before
    the chief priests he would be led?

Did she know when she welcomed the shepherds
    who came to call?
Did she know her son would be the greatest
    shepherd of all?

Did she know as she received the gifts from the kings
    who followed the eastern sky?
Did she know he would be the King of Kings and
    upon a cruel cross he would die?

Did she know as she wrapped him in swaddling
    clothes and cuddled him to her breast?
Did she know she would help wrap him at his death
    and in a tomb lay him to rest?

Did she know he would come out of that tomb
and reign the Triumphant King?
Did she know He would save so many lives,
for salvation He came to bring!

Did she know the significance of that first
Christmas day so many years ago?
Did she know? I wonder; with a heart
full of joy and sorrow, did she know?

A Serenity in My Heart

Goodness, it's a busy place outside my window
    in the early morning light.
There's plenty of seed for everyone little critters;
    you don't have to fight!

There come the mourning doves—for a symbol
    of peace they are quite aggressive,
But no match for the feisty squirrels—three
    this morning—each bossy and assertive!

The little brown sparrows grab a seed now
    and then from the bird feeder in the tree;
The red birds enjoy the bounty on the ground saying,
    "Thanks for sharing with me."

The rain gently falls from a gray sky leaving puddles
    for a really nice bird bath;
All this wonderful activity out my window warms
    my heart and makes me laugh!

I'm thankful for this quiet time and the beautiful scene
    in the early morning light,
Which helps create a serenity in my heart and whispers,
    "Everything will be all right!"

I've Walked with Jesus

On soft grassy paths I've walked with Jesus
    in little girl feet suntanned and bare;
On sandy paths I've walked with Jesus—just
    my foot prints, but I knew He was there.

On garden paths I've walked with Jesus as I
    remembered how in the garden He wept.
On sharp, rocky paths I've walked with Jesus
    as I slowly, carefully took each step.

I'm so glad I have walked life's path with Jesus
    since I was just a very little girl;
How quickly time has passed on this journey
    with Jesus; it's gone by in such a swirl!

The time is drawing nearer, Jesus, till I'll
    run with you down streets of gold.
Praising and thanking you, Precious Jesus,
    for the greatest love story ever told!

Family

I Remember That Boy

Come walk with me down memory lane;
    I have a sweet story to tell,
About the first time I met Willie's family;
    I remember that day very well.

My parents knew his parents because
    of a complicated family connection;
A little house, out in the country, across
    a babbling creek was our destination.

The house was built of wood and logs
    with a front porch kind of small;
Chairs were carefully arranged in the front yard–
    a welcome invite to all.

I remember a curly blonde headed little boy
    and two little girls about the age of me;
I also remember seeing something, or someone,
    way up in the branch of a tree!

There was a boy swinging on a rustic plane
    made of scraps of wood.
I thought "Wow, that is neat;
    I'd like to ride there with him if I could!"

Even though I was only five, I remember
    there was so much laughter and joy.
I remember that house and family; but most of all,
    I remember that boy!

    (I've been married to "that boy" for over 56 years!)

Mama's Sewing Room

Mama worked hours
    in that little sewing space,
Creating magic
    with a determined look on her face.
She'd take a selected fabric—
    a rectangular shape,
And turn it into a beautiful
    formal, curtain, or drape.

She had an image in her mind
    and a goal before her;
Pressure foot down and that
    ole "Singer" would whir.
I would stand and watch
    the magic come together:
Colorful cotton, satin and lace,
    even difficult leather.

Mama barely showed frustration
    when a needle would break,
Or when she had to use the seam ripper
    to fix a mistake.
Some people have a room for sewing;
    that's great if they are able.
My mom's sewing room
    was next to the kitchen table.

Oh, sweet memories I have of Mama
    in that special kitchen space,
As she created magic with a
    most determined look on her face!

Ironing Day

Happened on Tuesday most of the time
    since "washday" was on Monday.
Had to help Mama with the ironing before
    I could run outside and play.

Mama would carefully sprinkle the clothes
    before putting them in the refrigerator.
That way the clothes wouldn't sour if we had
    to iron them a little bit later.

We ironed jeans and shirts, dresses, blouses,
    and skirts—took us a while;
Mama and I would take turns at the ironing board—
    she with her pretty smile.

She taught me to do the sleeves and the collars
    and to carefully iron each cuff.
I don't know how many pieces of clothes
    we ironed each week, but it was enough!

I ironed a big basket of clothes for a lady
    who lived down the road just a little:
A sweet family with four kids and their parents,
    Benny and Betty Riddle.

She paid me $1.00 a dozen—that was a lot
    of money way back then;
The khaki shirts and gourd skirts were hard work,
    but that $7 brought a grin!

I ironed a shirt to wear to work this morning
    when these memories flooded my mind;
I really don't iron much anymore—most of my
    clothes are the "wash and wear" kind.

My mother taught her children to work hard;
    work always came before play.
Even though the work was tedious,
    I carry precious memories of "ironing day"!

The Trail to Grandma's House

There, in the woods, under the tall
    red oak and blackjack trees,
Stretches a beaten dirt path that lives
    in my treasured memories.

Bare feet made daily treks on this trail
    by a little girl and her brothers;
To share sweet communion with a kind
    twinkly-eyed grandmother.

The trail itself offered adventures
    for childhood make-believe;
To make tiny elf-hats and cups for fairies,
    there were acorns to retrieve.

There were rabbits, squirrels, birds,
    and wildflowers along the way;
It took a while to get to Grandma's—
    travel slowed by childhood play.

A warm hug awaited at the end
    of that well-worn path,
Where an imaginative, playful grandma
    was sure to make us laugh.

Bread and butter and sugar sandwiches
    were a delicious treat;
Listening to records with Grandma
    made the snacks extra sweet.

In my heart are many memories
    of a childhood of carefree fun;
The precious memory of the trail
    to Grandma's house is a special one.

My Grandma Souders babysat me each day while my mother worked. Grandma cooked at Johnson Elementary School and I went to work with her each day before I was old enough to go to school.

She passed away when I was seven but I've carried a part of her in my heart all of my life. My daddy's mother; a wonderful grandmother:

Velva Dee Souders
March 20, 1903–June 19,1957

Daddy's Strong Arms

Daddy and his fishing buddies went
    to the river to fish a while;
"I'm going to take Sissy with me,"
    Daddy told Momma with a smile.

I guess my five year old brothers—
    there were two of them you see—
Were more than daddy could handle
    So, he took three-year-old me.

I stayed close to my daddy's side;
    I loved him so.
I knew my daddy would keep me
    safe wherever I would go.

All afternoon I played on the river
    bank staying close to Daddy,
Until I heard these words, "Let's
    go home, Sissy, are you ready?"

So I ran across the river bank to
    Daddy's open arms…
Suddenly I started sinking and
    my heart pounded in alarm.

The little sandy puddle I had
    waded in with such glee
Pulled me quickly down;
    I was sinking past my knees.

I had never heard of quicksand—
    I was way too small;
But there, grinning down at me,
    stood my daddy so tall.

He reached down and with big strong
    arms he lifted me in the air.
My fear turned to joy; I had the biggest,
    strongest daddy anywhere.

I know my daddy's in Heaven and
    I will see him again someday;
I'm glad my Heavenly Father is with
    me in much the same way.

He has invited me to walk with Him
    along this path called life;
His eyes are always watching me through
    good times and times of strife.

Many times He has lifted me with
    His outstretched hand,
When I have felt myself sinking in the
    turmoil of life's quicksand.

I'm going to stay close to my Heavenly
    Father's side; I love Him so.
I know He will keep me safe through
    this life wherever I go.

The Calendar in the Hall

It hung on the east side of the hall
    right outside my bedroom door.
Every morning I would put an "X"
    over the date—the day after, one more.

I remember the number "222"—that's how
    many more days he would be gone;
Marking that calendar every day kept
    me going; but, I never felt so alone.

Our first baby girl was born during
    those calendar marking days;
I had to catch up on the "X's" as I was busy
    getting acquainted with her ways.

I would write long letters and give details
    of caring for this new life;
A new responsibility had been added
    to the role of being a sailor's wife.

His days were filled with duties on the ship
    as he counted days too.
I cherished his letters marked with "X's & O's"
    and "I Miss and Love You!"

At last, those long days of waiting
    came to an end;
Our baby girl got to meet her daddy—
    my best friend!

Many years have passed since that 19 year old
    stood staring at the wall,
Longingly marking off the days with an "X"
    on the calendar in the hall.

Life's Night Sounds

Tree frogs, crickets, coyotes yipping, drum beats
 from a powwow nearby,
Mama sweetly shushing baby sister
 when she would begin to cry.

Dogs barking, wind blowing, rain and hail pounding
 furiously all around;
Daddy wakes the family to go to the old cold
 damp cellar, safe underground.

Sirens blaring, horns honking, yells from harsh voices—
 city sounds new to a young bride;
Heart beating, softly breathing, joyfully snuggled
 next to her sweet sailor's side.

Precious baby wakes young mommy
 at the first little cry;
Loving mother singing softly, notes
 of a familiar lullaby.

Tense moments as the clock ticks minutes
 late into the night;
Relief at the sound of a car: "Young lady,
 this is just not right!"

Phone ringing: wakes sleeping household
 with a sense of urgency;
Mama's at the hospital with daddy—gotta go;
 it's an emergency.

Click, click, beep, beep, beep; you watch
    as the monitors keep a steady pace.
You want to scream in this ICU where it looks
    as if cancer will win the race.

Darkest is the night when your heart breaks
    with the loss of someone so dear;
Grief pours out of your soul, spilling on your
    pillow soaked with many a tear.

What's this joyful gathering of aunties, cousins,
    and friends late in the night?
Waiting, waiting, guessing what baby's weight
    will be—who will be right?

Congratulating sweet new parents—
    grandbabies bring so much joy;
They're a sweet reminder that life is a gift—
    each precious little girl and boy.

Tree frogs sing, crickets chirp, coyotes yip
    at the golden moon;
Sweet silver haired husband snores softly,
    old age came way too soon.

Life's night sounds will go on for generations,
    as new branches are added to the tree;
With joy and sorrow mixed together, strong families
    continue, the way it was meant to be.

Watermelon Summer

Early Spring: time to get the field ready,
    lots of work to do;
Hope to reap a juicy harvest before
    the summer's through.

Build a fence around the land—
    about two acres or more,
Lots of wire and post—several trips
    to the hardware store.

Shop around for a tractor—
    wanted one since he was a boy,
Shiny new orange Kubota—
    better than a new Christmas toy.

Troublesome bermuda, maybe should
    wait until next year;
Troublesome bermuda, maybe
    won't plant anything here.

Spray paint marks the twelve foot
    distance to plant the seed,
Good space between the rows to plow
    up any intruding weed.

Trip to the seed store—dreaming
    of those watermelons so sweet:
Charleston Gray, Black Diamonds,
    Jubilee, and Yellow Meat.

Need to buy some fertilizer before
    the shopping trip is through;
Don't forget cantaloupe seed—need
    to plant a few of those too.

Wait a little while to plant; let the field
   be warmed by the sun,
Teamwork–dropping seed and fertilizer
   gets the planting done.

Check every few days to see
   if the watermelon will sprout;
Finally, all over the field, tiny
   green plants are peeking out.

Disc between the rows, hoe the weeds,
   pray for rain and wait.
What a beautiful sight, those little
   flowers on rows so straight.

Scorching sun beating down,
   we worry the plants will die,
Please God, send us rain–it's so hot,
   the good soil is so dry.

"Should we irrigate?" a conversation
   in the middle of the night;
To lose this crop after all this hard work
   just doesn't seem right.

A prayer and a search for a scripture–
   this one jumps right out at me:
"I will give you abundant water for
   your parched fields," Isaiah 44:3.

Plant a tiny seed of faith in our hearts
   and read that verse every day;
God really is in control of the weather;
   quit worrying, relax, and pray.

How we wanted to sing and dance
   when the showers would come;
Every time the field needed a good watering,
   God would send some.

From the beginning of time, man has
    celebrated the joy of the harvest;
Enjoying the fruits of our labor, we celebrated
    too, and felt very blessed.

Sisters and brothers came to help,
    gathering the crop a family affair;
How fun to look out over the field
    and see so much help everywhere.

We loaded them in the front-end-loader
    and put them in the pickup;
We loaded them in a big trailer and hauled
    them to market by a big truck.

We picked them early every day before
    the sun would get too hot;
We looked for a place for a watermelon
    stand until we found a perfect spot.

Our days have been filled with watermelon;
    what a summer it has been,
Watching girls and boys as sweet juice
    dripped from each little chin.

We forgot how much we worked and worried;
    it just seemed like play.
We've sold them, eaten all we wanted,
    and we've given many away.

The field is looking kind of barren now,
    the end of the season is near;
Good-bye sweet watermelon summer,
    hope to see you again next year!

Written in the summer of 2006; the best watermelon summer ever.

Hearing Grandpa Pray

I walked to Grandpa's house—
    thought I'd visit for a while;
But, I stopped outside his door
    and listened with a smile.

Grandpa wasn't alone
    that sunny summer day;
Grandpa was talking to God,
    I know 'cause I heard him pray.

Grandpa was praying in a Heavenly
    language to his Father above,
And Grandpa's prayer
    was full of faith and love.

Grandpa's prayer was powerful
    as his voice rang out so clear;
And I could sense the presence
    of God very near.

I listened a while before
    I quietly slipped away;
But I'll never forget
    hearing Grandpa pray.

Now Grandpa was a preaching man
    and I often heard him preach;
Grandpa was a teaching man
    and I often heard him teach.

Grandpa was a guitar man
    and I often heard him play;
Grandpa was a joking man
    with funny things to say.

Grandpa was a singing man
    who loved to sing a song,
And Grandpa was a man of faith
    who tried to do no wrong.

These memories I carry with me
    and many more,
Since God called Grandpa
    to Heaven's shore.

But the thing I remember most
    to this very day,
Was Grandpa talking to God;
    I know 'cause I heard him pray.

Rev. W. W. Yoder, known to me as "Grandpa", pastored the Johnson Church of God during the 1940's. After Grandpa retired from pastoring other churches in Oklahoma, he moved back to the Johnson community. He lived in a little gray house next to the church. It was in that little house that this precious memory was made.

Golden Lessons

Mother and Daddy,

You thought you were just building a house
    the year I was five,
But you were teaching your kids one of the many
    lessons you would weave into our lives.
You were teaching us to make plans
    and to follow through,
You were teaching us how to make
    dreams come true.

Daddy,

The day you committed your life to the Lord–
    the year I was seven;
You may have thought it was between you and God,
    but you were teaching your children about Heaven.
And Daddy, you may have thought you were buying books
    for your own enjoyment at that old estate.
But, you were teaching your children to value books
    the year that I was eight.

Mother,

As you cleaned and baked and sewed and reminded us,
    "Kids, do your chores."
You thought you were just keeping a busy household
    going, but you were doing so much more.
You were teaching us how to care for a family,
    the many things there are to do.
You were teaching us lessons that will go
    with us all our lives through.

And Daddy,

Remember how in front of our house
    cars would get stuck,
When the rain would turn our road
    into knee deep mud and muck?
You thought you were just starting the tractor
    to help a neighbor,
But you were teaching us to help others in need
    with our labor.

Daddy and Mother,

Adopting every stray animal that came
    on the place; in this fashion
I think you taught us kids something
    about compassion.
The laughter and love we have shared
    during holidays has led to the conviction
There's something precious
    about establishing family traditions.
You've taught us the value of family
    and to the church to show reverence;
You've taught us to work hard
    and the value of perseverance.
You've taught us to value life,
    and you've taught us
How the love should be between
    a husband and a wife.
As you celebrate the love that
    has endured for a decade of five,
Thank you for weaving these
    Golden Lessons into our lives.

I wrote this for my parents and read it at their 50th anniversary reception: August 16, 1996.

Daddy Planted an Orchard

"Daddy," I said when I was a
    just a little girl so high,
"My favorite dessert in the world
    is cherry pie."

With love in his voice
    and a gleam in his eye,
"I'll see what I can do about that,"
    was his reply.

Daddy may have bought a pie,
    or Mama may have made one,
But the thing I remember the
    most that was so much fun:

Daddy planted an orchard.

He didn't plant just one cherry tree,
    and he didn't plant just two;
For my daddy's generous heart,
    that wouldn't do.

He planted rows and rows of what
    looked like twigs to me,
And we dreamed how beautiful
    the cherry orchard would be.

As time tends to do,
    the years have flown;
And the love and admiration
    for my daddy has grown.

My mind wanders back
    to that little grove of trees
Where I walked beside
    my daddy dreaming of cherries.

I remember the lessons Daddy
	taught his family along the way,
Lessons planted in our hearts
	that are so difficult to convey.

Lessons planted because…
	Daddy planted an orchard.

In Daddy's Orchard:

He planted a sense of adventure—
	that life was meant to be fun;
He planted a sense of justice—
	but not to judge anyone.

He planted the value of patriotism;
	to his country he was devoted.
He respected the Flag and
	he always got out and voted.

He planted in his family a sense
	of pride and integrity,
He planted the importance
	of compassion and generosity.

He planted in our hearts
	what it means to be loyal,
And he planted how to have strength
	during times of turmoil.

He planted the importance of prayer
	in everything you do;
He planted faith in God's Word:
	the strength that will sustain you.

My daddy, our daddy, brother,
	grandpa, and friend,

His life on this earth
    has come to an end,
But the love he planted
    will continue to grow,
Because so much love was planted;
    this I know!

Some people plant seeds
    and some people plant trees,
But when it comes to the love
    that Daddy leaves:

    Daddy planted an orchard!

I wrote this poem and read it at my daddy's funeral December 12, 2007.

Delbert James Souders
May 28, 1924-December 8, 2007

The Old Iron Bed Frame

It seemed to speak to me in the
    silent cold night;
I spotted it over in the tall grass
    as it reflected the moonlight.

Just part of an old iron bed frame,
    but it had so much to say—
Of babies being born, and families
    kneeling at night to pray.

Of an old feather bed where handmade
    quilts warmed weary ones;
Where mommies cuddled sweet baby
    girls and precious little sons.

Where families gathered to share precious
    time before a final goodbye.
Where pillows were wet with lonely tears
    as broken hearts were left to cry.

Our daughter was hurting and we had
    to come to see what we could do;
There was turmoil and sadness from
    wrong choices—we've all made a few.

And there, in the dark, as I prayed for
    wisdom, in this tough circumstance,
I saw it—that old bed frame—and, at first, I
    just gave it a mindless glance.

Then, I thought how things are sometimes
        happy and sometimes sad,
And how God gives us the strength to keep
        going when things look really bad.

"That's the way it is in life," the old bed
        frame said to me in the still cold night.
"You will get through the tough times and,
        with faith, everything will be alright."

Prelude to a Poem

I sat right down with pen in hand
    and thought I'd write a rhyme.
It's fun to do and not too hard;
    just have to find the time.

This poem—these words cascading
    across the blue lined page—
This poem must be special because
    tonight I have a stage.

I get to stand in front of folks
    that will listen to my voice.
I said, "Sure!" when Garry asked me—
    it was really an easy choice.

"Now what will I say?" I asked myself
    to this audience unknown to me;
I've got to write something special—
    I must choose my words carefully.

I thought a while and then decided
    I'll write about no other;
Today I'll write a special poem
    and dedicate it to my brother.

I'll write about treasured childhood
    memories, Garry, so you will know
How much I loved growing up with
    you so many years ago!

*I wrote this June 18, 2015, before attending A poetry reading at
Benedict Street Market.*

To Garry with Love

The year was 1946; the war had ended and
    our daddy took our mama to be his bride.
Just a little over a year later, they welcomed
    their twin baby boys with pride.

Mama was only eighteen,
    Daddy was twenty-three,
Then just two years
    later they welcomed me.

Mama took care of two little boys and
    a little baby daughter,
In an old farmhouse with no electricity
    or running water.

For three little country kids growing up
    in the 50's, life was sweet;
We never knew how hard Mama and Daddy
    worked to make sure we had plenty to eat.

We attended a little country schoolhouse
    with boxed suppers and Christmas plays.
There was such a strong sense of community;
    that's the way it was in those days.

Mr. and Mrs. Cheek taught readin', writin',
    and 'rithmatic, and to obey the Golden Rule.
(They lived in the little "teacherage" across
    the road from the school.)

Garry and Larry shot BB guns, climbed trees,
    and played baseball.
They built me playhouses under those trees
    where I played with my dolls.

Our baby sister came along and completed
    the family in '58;
I finally had a baby sister—it had been
    a very long wait.

We swam in cow ponds and ran carefree
    through the woods.
We rode horses with our friends;
    life was really pretty good.

We grew up learning that
    hard work was a virtue—
And there was always
    plenty of hard work to do.

Larry and Garry milked the cows and
    plowed with a team of mules.
I cooked, sewed, and washed dishes;
    We didn't question our parents' rules.

Now the decade of the 60's came and
    High School was a blast;
Those good ole Earlsboro High School
    years went way too fast.

Carefree highschool days turned to
    a war that weighed heavy on our heart;
We all married young but military duties
    pulled young couples apart.

Time went so quickly, and suddenly
    we were grown;
Before we knew it, we all had children
    of our own.

How I treasure the memories of
    us growing up together;
How I treasure how you have always
    been my big brother.

Thank you for helping your little sister
    along the way,
And thank you for spending this special
    time with me today.

In June of 2015, Garry invited me to attend a "Poetry Reading" at Benedict Street Marketplace, and he asked me to bring a poem to read.

I decided to surprise Garry with an original poem written just for him. The joyful look on his face as I read this poem is a treasure I will always carry in my heart.

A Little Gold Band

A very small girl once said
    to her mother,
"Mama, you know who I would be
    if I could be another?"

"I would be a pretty lady
    with very soft skin,
With big blue eyes and
    a dainty little chin."

"I would have small hands
    so soft and feminine,
And Mama, you know what would
    be on the finger of one hand?"

"On one finger there would be
    a pretty little ring,
A little ring Mama—
    A little gold band."

"I would be a lady with soft curls,
    blonde hair, brown, red, or black,
Long hair, though, with curls that
    would hang down my back."

"When I would walk, my walk
    would be a gentle walk Mama…lovely,
And my voice would be soft and full of love,"
    said the little girl wistfully.

I would have lots of nice things, the prettiest
    things, Mama, in all the land,
But my nicest thing would be a pretty little ring,
    Mama, a little gold band."

"And Mama, everybody would love me,
    everybody would love this lady I want to be,
Because she would love everybody and she would
    be so good, and so happy."

"Then someday, this lady I want to be
    would meet someone to love and marry.
You know what I mean, Mama, like you and Daddy.
    Mama, do you understand me?"

"He would take me lots of places,
    and I would wear the finest laces,
He would buy me lots of nice things—
    The prettiest things in all the land."

"But, Mama, do you know what
    the nicest thing would be?
Do you know what he would
    buy special for me?"

"The very nicest thing would be a ring
    to wear on one finger of my hand,
A little ring, Mama,
    a little gold band."

The little girl's mother gently lifted
    a dainty little chin,
and looked in soft blue eyes, happiness
    and love shining from within.

She smoothed down soft little curls,
    as she softly replied to her little girl,
"I wouldn't worry about the beauty
    you wish for,
And even if you're not rich,
    you will never be poor."

"I think this lady you will be,
    will be loved and will be happy.
But, about the little ring,
    to you it seems the most important thing,
I only pray that somewhere in this land
    there is a boy who will deserve to give you
That little gold band!"

I wrote this poem in 1968 when I was a romantic 18 year old, living in Long Beach, California, with my sweet husband, Willie, who was in the Navy.

In 1995, our daughter, Sarah Pryor, displayed a framed copy of this poem at her wedding reception.

The Patchwork Days of Our Lives

The patchwork days of a woman's life
    pieced together make a pattern of beauty and joy,
From the very first cry when the doctor smiles
    at Dad and says, "It's not a boy!"

It's not "Snips and snails and puppy dog tails,"
    but it's tears and laughter and giggles and wails.
It's an emotional bundle with energy galore;
    life is never boring when you're born a girl!

Wrapped up in your quilt
    and taken home to enjoy,
Your parents will never regret
    that you were not a boy.

Those baby days end so quickly
    of diaper and bib;
Before you know it, you're
    climbing out of that crib.

The first patch of your life comes
    to an end and baby days are no more,
But, oh, the fun has just begun for the
    "toddler days" are fun galore!

You run and play and laugh and giggle
    with your baby quilt close by.
You're independent or clingy, messy
    or neat, outgoing or shy.

You turn around a time or two
    and a toddler you are no more.
You're a little girl ready for school,
    and now what fun is in store!

There's jump ropes and crayons
    and holding hands with a friend.
When you're a little girl,
    the fun just never seems to end.

But, at nap time, you'll need the comfort
    of your patchwork friend,
Which by now Mom's had to wash
    several times—and mend!

The days pass so quickly;
    time passing in a whirl.
Before you know it your
    no longer a little girl.

But you are make-up and clothes
    and staying up late.
You're a teen age girl ready
    for your first date.

You carry your security
    with no guilt.
There in your purse is a remnant
    of that baby quilt.

Time passes and your best friend is no longer
    the giggling teen-age girl by your side,
For now you have a lifetime friend;
    you are a bride!

You'll need something new, something blue,
    and a penny in your shoe;
And tucked in your Bible
    in a careful fold,
There's no doubt what
    you'll carry that's old!

Now, you're a mom and juggling is an art,
    but you manage to do it fine,
Because your mother and her mother juggled too;
    we do it all the time.

There's housework, kids, laundry, and jobs;
    there's school, church, and more.
For this patch in your patch-work life,
    you'll need energy galore!

Carefully placed in a memory box
    is a ragged piece of your life.
You rarely have time to look at it now;
    you are so busy being a mother and a wife.

But, your little baby quilt is there as a reminder
    of the security of God, family, and friends;
Now you make quilts for your babies and grandbabies,
    for the love of family never ends!

And you pass the days sometimes in such a craze,
    with life in such a swirl.
But God gave you the ability to do many things
    because He made you a girl.

Your patchwork life from all your days
    make such an interesting design.
With the security of God's love sewn in each patch,
    Wherever He leads you, you will do just fine.

I wrote this poem in September, 2000, and dedicate it to all the girls in
the family. Two little girls especially loved their baby quilts: our niece,
Janel Souders, and our daughter, Sarah McAfee Pryor.

Daddy Played the Harmonica

Daddy played the harmonica.
    I thought about that today,
While listening to the Bellamy Brothers
    and the instruments they play.

I've heard three versions of "He's an
    Old Hippie", and I love each song.
I can just imagine if any of us "oldies"
    hear one, we have to sing along.

My daddy loved music; he especially seemed
    to enjoy songs from the sixties.
He liked Bob Dylan, Simon & Garfunkel,
    and Willie Nelson–I think he
        was an "Old Hippie."

He really wasn't an "Old Hippie" but he was
    a free thinker and wise in so many ways.
I loved his positive attitude, and I loved the way he
    played the harmonica back in the olden days!

Boo and Baby

She was the cutest little blue-eyed baby,
    a prayer answered I do believe;
A precious real live baby doll to love,
    brought home on Christmas Eve.

She showed spunk and determination
    from the very start,
And she, our little sister, had a way of
    winning everyone's heart.

She was entertaining and delightful
    and if you watched her play,
It would have been obvious that
    she would be a nurse someday.

If she wasn't wrapping bandages
    around her poor felines,
She was practicing giving shots
    to her baby doll's behinds.

She worked at different jobs
    through her teen years,
But the nursing home job probably
    started her career.

She went to college determined
    to get a nursing degree,
But, she got so much more;
    was it destiny?

She met him in January;
    was it love at first sight?
Maybe so, because everything
    just seemed so right.

He was a college student also
    and worked at a service station;
It was there they planned
    their wedding celebration.

They found they had a lot in common
    during those "get acquainted days",
And they learned they shared some
    of the same stubborn ways.

They were both articulate, friendly,
    outgoing, and smart;
It really did seem they were meant to be
    from the very start.

They married in June— a handsome groom,
    and a beautiful bride;
How pretty she looked as she walked
    down the aisle by her daddy's side.

They honeymooned in Eureka Springs
    and started married life together;
He worked hard to help her achieve the
    nursing degree we all treasure.

They decided to start a family—a child
    would bring them joy;
Finally after seven long years, they
    had their precious baby boy.

Kelly taught high school math,
    tutored, and tenderly guided his son;
Cindy spent hours taking care of patients,
    but always had time for her little one.

A shining star to his mom and dad,
    Nicolas has been their pride and joy;
When he delivered the Valedictory address
    they both beamed, "That's our boy!"

They have had twenty-five busy
    years together,
Working side by side
    encouraging each other.

Though the going has not always been easy—
    life is just not that way;
They have put God first in their marriage,
    and, He has been their strength for each day.

My precious sister, my Christmas doll
    that I love so,
I'm glad you found your "Boo" and
    he found his "Baby" twenty-five years ago!

I wrote this poem for my sister and brother-in-law, Cynthia and Kelly Chancellor, for their 25th wedding anniversary, June 12, 2006

The House That Love Built

There's a song about the house that
    love built and I love it so;
I guess because I live in the house
    my daddy built a long time ago.

I was five when daddy first framed
    this house and hung each rafter;
Now six generations have filled these
    rooms with love and laughter.

From my Grandpa John to my great
    grandson—a family to treasure;
The precious memories made in this
    house are without measure.

There, in the kitchen, is where Mother
    taught me how to flute a pie;
There, in that bedroom, Garry hung
    my doll and made me cry.

There, next to the fireplace, grandkids
    would perform a song;
In the same room, using Cindy's caroling
    books we all sang along.

There's where we played card games
    and long hours of Monopoly;
Me and my wonderful ornery brothers,
    The twins—Larry and Garry.

There, on the west side of the house,
  Willie stole his first kiss.
There's where I realized we were being
  spied on by my little sis!

There's where my nervous boyfriend asked
  my dad if he could marry me;
Our reception was held in this house with
  a wedding cake so very pretty.

I don't dwell on the past; there's new
  memories to make each day.
Yet, it's fun reminiscing in the house where
  the "little girl me" used to play.

There's a song about the house that love built,
  no wonder I love it so;
I live in a house that love built, and where
  love continues to grow.

If the Old House Could Talk

If that old abandoned house could talk,
    I wonder what it would say,
About the folks that worked and played
    before they went away.

I wonder about the folks that sat on that
    back porch; I wonder what was said.
Did the Momma tell the kids to snap the beans,
    while she went in to make the bread?

Did big sister rock the baby and watch for
    Daddy to walk across the yard?
Did little brother play without a worry in
    the world, or was life really hard?

There, in the upstairs bedroom, where
    curtains hang ragged and torn,
Sits an old dusty steamer trunk, completely
    empty—its appearance forlorn.

From where did that trunk travel and what
    precious treasure did it hold?
Did it come by boat or train with worldly
    possessions of a dreamer bold?

Who built you old house, who hammered
    the nails and hung the rafters?
Did a family grow together here and share
    lots of love and laughter?

You have been empty for so long; if you
    could speak, what would you say?
Please tell me, old house, about the people
    who lived in you before they went away!

Daddy's Bible

Each moment as I walk through the day,
I am strengthened by faith in such a strong way.
And, I feed that faith as much as I am able,
Reading my daddy's Bible at the kitchen table.

Now, Daddy read this Bible with joy in his heart,
And "Wonderful Words of Life" it did impart.
It comforted him each day when he was sad,
And added to his joy when he was glad.

This Bible was read, and lived, by this Godly man,
Who believed in the importance of following God's plan.
Faith and family gave my daddy purpose in life,
And, oh, how he loved his children and his wife.

Daddy left treasured memories and a heritage of love,
And he made sure I knew I had a Heavenly Father above.
He quietly told me, before he left this earthly home,
"Keep the family together and keep your faith strong."

If Daddy could look down from Heaven, he would see
I am doing my best to follow the lessons he taught me.
And, I feed that faith, as much as I am able,
Reading my daddy's Bible at the kitchen table.

Thinking

Thinking about my loving husband;
I'm so blessed to be his wife.
Thinking about children and grandchildren,
And other precious family in my life.
Thinking about wonderful friends,
I've met so many dear folks along the way.
It's the people y'all—the greatest gift
God places in our life each and every day!

That's what I've been thinking this morning!

Janie Elizabeth

We have a little girl
    named Janie Elizabeth;
Who, I must confess
    is quite a little mess!

She thinks she must have her way
    every night and every day.
She would rather throw a fit
    than to quietly sit.

But, oh how sweet she can be
    when she cuddles next to me,
And says "umm umm dood"
    the way a lovin' baby should.

After she's all bathed
    and dressed for bed,
I hold her close and
    caress that little curly head,

And thank God above
    for this little mess—
Our precious little girl
    Janie Elizabeth!

I wrote this poem February 19, 1980. Janie, our fourth baby girl, turned 2 on March 10, 1980.

Two Happy Fishermen

Willie made it home—smile on his face;
He and Melvin found the right fishin' place.

Willie carried home a big bag of catfish filets;
This has been the best "fish were bitin' days".

I can just see those two brothers, each with a big grin,
Out in the middle of the lake throwing their lines in.

Willie said the fish didn't just nibble, they "hit and run".
I know those two ole fishermen had so much fun!

Late last night the cast iron skillet was sizzlin' hot;
Those delicious catfish filets really hit the spot.

There are a lot more fish to have at a later date;
Probably a Sunday fish fry—I can hardly wait.

So glad Willie made it home with a smile on his face;
So glad he and Melvin found the right fishin' place!

August 21, 2015, after a very successful fishing trip.

Road Trip

"On the road again…" My Willie sings
    a little of the song,
While I read poetry out loud;
    I brought some books along.

We are a happy couple,
    so fun to get away;
Hoeing watermelons and housework
    can wait another day.

We are good company for each other—
    have been for a while;
He is funny in this setting—
    always makes me smile.

He points out scenic pictures—
    tells me to take a look;
I try so hard to keep my nose
    out of a book.

We reminisce about familiar
    landmarks along the way;
It's nice to be comfortable in silence;
    no words we need to say.

He sings a silly song about the pitter patter
    of little tires on the "rub board" highway;
I dramatically articulate words from Longfellow
    in my expressive "not so shy" way.

Blue skies, sunshine,
    joy we cannot measure;
On a road trip,
    making memories to treasure.

A Little Girl to Love

Mommy, Daddy, and big sisters too
Eagerly wait until the ultrasound is through;
What is that image in the monitor above?
Sarah and Rodney, you are going to have
    Another little girl to love.

Waiting room full of family and friends:
Big sisters, grandmas, grandpas, aunts, and
Uncles—the list just doesn't seem to end.
How much longer? What did you say?
Baby Ayla is on the way!
Finally, wrapped in a blanket as soft as a dove.
Hey everyone, we have
    Another little girl to love.

Text messages sent, phone calls made,
Pictures taken of all that dark hair,
Well, there's just not a sweeter baby
In all the world—not anywhere!
Let me see her; please don't shove.
How exciting everyone, we have
    Another little girl to love.

A beautiful baby, a precious gift
Sent from Heaven above.
Thank you Heavenly Father
For sending us
    Another little girl to love!

Ayla Breanne Pryor, our fifth granddaughter, joined our family on August 31, 2009.

Those Canyons

Those Canyons....
   Loved them as a child
We yelled and hollered
   Pretty much ran wild.

Didn't know there
   Was a world out there;
Just surrounded by nature
   Not a single care.

Daddy bought the 80 acres
   When I was a little girl;
Those growing up years
   Passed in such a swirl.

We four children, our children,
   And their children too,
Found joy in exploring this land;
   So much to do.

Now, my son comes home
   Talking about his canyon hideout,
And the yummy food he cooked–
   So much better than "take out".

Yep, I love those canyons, the pond,
   The open field and each beautiful tree.
A place away from the world,
   What a beautiful place to be.

Willie's Haircut

"I sure need a haircut,"
    Willie has been saying for a while.
"I'll make you an appointment,"
    I said with a smile.

"No," came his answer, "I won't make
    an appointment," said Willie.
"Ok, just let it grow then," I said,
    "Though I think you're being silly."

The frequency of this hair conversation
    has been ongoing;
And Willie's pretty silver hair has kept
    on growing and growing.

Until today!

I asked my sweet hubby what he needed
    before I made a Walmart run;
"A haircut kit," was his reply.
    I thought, "This will be fun!"

So I bought the kit and sent a text
    to Sarah, our daughter dear;
"Hey, your dad is in desperate need
    of a haircut; can you come here?"

Now, Sarah is a therapist and a
    mighty fine one, I will have to say.
She's not a barber, but I thought
    she could surely give it a try today.

So she did come and she clipped
    and clipped—she took her time;
She did a good job and her silver-
    haired Daddy looked just fine.

Willie got a good haircut today!

We laughed during this haircut experience
    and now Sarah has a new name;
She is a "Hairapist"– aren't all
    beauticians and barbers the same?

They listen to your problems and stories
    while they cut your hair.
Sometimes they offer advice—I guess
    there are "Hairapists" everywhere!

Now, handsome Willie won't need
    a haircut for a while;
"I'll come when I'm needed,"
    Sarah said with a smile.

We won't have to worry about Willie
    getting a haircut anymore—
Not since I bought that haircut kit
    from the Walmart store!

(And hair won't tickle Willie's ears anymore!)

My Kids

On a trip to Walmart this morning
        I thought it would be neat
To take some goodies to my students—
        A special treat.

Willie helped me carry groceries in
        and he asked, "What's this for?"
(As he helped me carry ice, pop,
        and chips through the door.)

"My Kids," I said.
        I love the sound of those words!
                "My Kids!"

My kids are mommies, daddies,
        veterinarians, and teachers;
My kids are police officers, store clerks,
        child care workers, and preachers.

My kids work in offices, on ranches, or
        in a department store;
My kids are mechanics, machinists,
        electricians, and more.

My kids have been on mission trips
        to Africa and other places;
My kids have been on sports teams
        and have run marathon races.

My kids have served in every branch
    of the military—it's true!
My kids have been musicians, artists,
    authors, and illustrators too.

Some of my kids that walked through
    the classroom door,
Left us too soon and now walk with Jesus
    on Heaven's shore.

For just a few months they came into my
    classroom and they were mine;
My students—to teach, to encourage,
    to inspire, and to love all the time.

All different, all amazing, all with a reason
    for being here—God's design;
Once again I stand before a group of kids
    and say, "This year you are mine!"

"My Kids!"
    I love the sound of those words;
I love being a teacher!
    I love "My Kids!"

After being retired for a year, my heart longed to be back in the classroom.
I wrote this poem in August, 2021, after I started teaching again.

The Heart of a Two Year Old

In the heart of a two year old there is
    so much to learn and do.
They don't know much about the world yet;
    that's up to me and you.

They're exploring their world as they run and
    play with a smile on their face.
They need to be guided with love and patience;
    they need a safe place.

When they spill something, or grab a marker
    and write on the wall,
Please respond with kindness and
    remember they are still very small!

Oh, that each tender little one could have
    caring adults in his or her life,
Where the little one is tenderly guided
    without harshness or strife.

In the heart of a little two year old,
    there is so much to learn and do.
They don't know much about the world yet;
    that's up to me and you!

This poem was inspired by our precious grandson, River Jacobs Pryor, who was two at the time the poem was written on July 8, 2019.

Willie Loves Cars

Willie loves cars; I learned
    that a long time ago.
I knew it as his young bride when
    he bought that '68 GTO.

We've had old cars, new cars,
    pick-up trucks and more;
We especially loved the '66 Mustang
    that took a while to restore.

Of all the vehicles we have owned
    the yellow roadster was by far
One of my and Willie's favorites
    "So much fun to drive" car!

The Chrysler Crossfire is a six speed
    and it wants to get up and go!
The speedometer says it will do "160"
    but Willie says, "No!"

We took it on a Sunday drive to
    Wewoka Lake one day;
A special place where he and
    his siblings used to play.

The little yellow roadster is a keeper;
    at least I hope so.
Yep, Willie loves cars; I learned that
    A long time ago!

The Cake That Grew

For birthday number four, Sugar Baby
    wanted a "Paw Patrol" cake.
I thought to myself, "I believe that is
    something I can make!"

Now, part of it has to be gluten free for
    our little princess to eat;
Two special cake mixes would make the
    top layer yummy and sweet.

You have to think about perspective for
    it to please the eyes;
It took three cake mixes for the bottom
    layer to be the right size.

When it all came together, iced with a
    decorator frosting recipe,
It turned out a little bigger than this cake
    maker thought it would be.

The smile on Brooklyn's face when she
    first saw her special cake,
Made it worthwhile—the time it took
    to mix, bake, and decorate.

So the Paw Patrol delicacy fed a bunch
    of skaters at a party so fine;
And we will probably be eating leftover
    cake for a very long time!

The Breakfast Picnic

We packed a little bit of food,
    this little lady and me;
Thought we'd have a breakfast
    picnic under a tree.

A good hike from the house
    we found a pretty place;
We spread out a tablecloth
    with a smile on our face.

I enjoyed my toast and peanut butter
    and a cup of morning brew;
Brooklyn had packed cereal, milk,
    and an Instant Breakfast too.

She found the tiniest snail
    to hold in her hand and adore;
She's such a busy little girl
    with a great big world to explore.

She spilled her Instant Breakfast
    with her busy little feet;
"That's ok, Brooklyn, you still
    have a bowl of cereal to eat."

There was a monster in the trees
    that needed chased away,
So, "Busy Feet" spilled the cereal–
    "Hmm, what will you eat today?"

"I know, let's find a melon
    in the field for me and you;
Don't you think that would
    be a wonderful thing to do?"

It gave me a chance to teach her
    about the flowering plants that bite;
You have to be careful—those stinging
    nettles you do not want to fight.

We crisscrossed the field, being careful
    as we took each step;
Then we found a ripe melon…
    splat, crack! Was it good? Yep!

Our breakfast picnic was so much fun;
    we sang, we talked, we ate!
Maybe we will do this again someday;
    I can hardly wait!

Artist in Residence

Dear Cousin Claudia came for a visit
    and we all enjoyed her stay;
She provided paint, brushes, canvases,
    and guidance in our home yesterday.

Beautiful colors danced around Oklahoma
    windmills created at my table!
Guided by our teacher, we became artists—
    even those who did not think we were able.

Sometimes quiet contemplation, sometimes
    laughter, sometimes a word of advise,
We created special memories that will always
    be treasured; the afternoon was so nice!

Thank you, Dear Cousin, for helping
    create such a wonderful day!
Thank you, Heavenly Father, for her gift
    and for sending her our way!

Great Strength in Love

I step out on my porch
　　in the early morning light,
And my heart is filled with joy
　　at this beautiful sight:

Chairs arranged in different areas,
　　one there, these three in a row;
All symbols of a wonderful family
　　who gathered a couple days ago.

Oh, we had some good discussions—
　　we certainly did not all agree,
But we are stronger than disagreements;
　　we are a strong family!

My focus shifts to the flag:
　　The Red, White, and Blue.
This symbol of our Country
　　brings joy to my heart too.

We may be in some heated discussions—
　　on different sides we take a stand,
Because we have different ideas
　　of what makes this Country grand.

I pray we remain stronger than differences
　　and seek guidance from above;
And may we always remember this truth,
　　"There is great strength in love!"

Friends

The Quilting Bee

Several little girls giggling with glee,
Stitching and talking at the quilting bee.
Grandmas and friends showing them the way
Quilts were made in the olden' days.

"I need help threading my needle," said one.
While another happily replied, "This is fun!"
The quilting frames held patches so bright,
Everyone tried to make their stitches just right.

Now Grandma Wanda wanted the girls to know
How to "tack" a quilt together–no stitches to sew;
The material was bought–a pattern with hearts;
We needed batting and lining before we could start.

On the quilting frame was stretched the lining;
On top of that came the soft white quilt batting.
On the outside the heart material would show;
Together the three layers we would carefully sew.

The yarn would be cut into lengths to tie;
Some of the girls were a little hesitant to try.
But with practice, each of them made a knot,
(Alma's leadership was appreciated a lot!)

Mertie, Helen, Wanda, and others led the way,
Teaching the "Joy Belles" lessons about the olden' days,
In a little church where everyone giggled with glee
Stitching and talking at the Quilting Bee.

Maggie

I named her Maggie and she and I have
    become such good friends;
She stands there proud and strong even in the
    harshest of Oklahoma winds.

She creates a wonder in my spirit;
    like Joyce Kilmer I would have to agree;
There have been many a poem written;
    yet, not one as lovely as this tree.

She was planted by my daddy's hands
    at least fifty years ago;
Through all these years, I have delighted
    in watching her grow.

Once, wind chimes made the prettiest melody
    as tiny metal spikes clinked together;
The chimes met their fate when they became tangled
    due to stormy weather.

There are scars in her bark where many a nail
    was driven to form a ladder;
Tree houses were built by rambunctious boys;
    to her it did not seem to matter.

Her leaves are thick—a waxy green; they grow
    in clusters of various hues.
She doesn't seem to mind with the gentlest of
    a breeze, many a leaf she will lose.

She has the most beautiful fragrant blossoms—
  white and silky to the touch,
Nobility, perseverance, love of nature—symbols
  of this majestic tree convey so much!

In the cool mornings, I rake her leaves that
  have gently cascaded to the ground;
In her shade, I feel the peaceful presence
  of our Creator all around.

I named her Maggie—short for Magnolia, of course;
  and it's very plain to see,
She, with deep roots, strong branches, and delicate
  blossoms is a friend to me.

A Reminder From My Feathered Friends

They skitter, they scatter, they hop they fly;
    they have so much to do.
There are red ones, blue ones, and the tiniest
    little gray and black ones too.

I wonder if they know their Heavenly Father
    has promised to give them what they need.
(God allowed me to be His instrument
    as I threw them several handfuls of seed.)

I began to focus my mind on challenges
    this morning and wrinkle my brow in worry,
Then I caught a glimpse of my feathered friends,
    and I decided not to get in a hurry.

I sat here and thought about His love for me
    and His promises—there are so many.
So promises, or problems? What will you pick up?
    Of both, there are plenty!

They skitter, they scatter, they hop, they fly,
    and they seem to talk to me too,
"Hang on to His promises; He will take care of us,
    and He will take care of you!"

Come on Over Neighbor

Come on over neighbor,
    and sit awhile.
We'd like to share some time with you;
    we'd like to see your smile.

We are all so busy rushin' around—
    off to work, to church, and such;
We pass each other on the road,
    but don't have time to visit much.

We look after each other though
    as we rush through our busy day;
We always stop to help our neighbor
    'cause that's the country way.

Movin' dirt, diggin' ditches,
    roundin' up a stray goat or horse—
"Could you look after the place while I'm gone?"
    The answer's always, "Of course!"

We are so blessed, neighbor;
    we know you realize it too.
Isn't it fun livin' right here
    in our woodsy country zoo?

Did you hear the coyotes
    yelpin' in the night?
Did you see the wild turkeys
    and the geese in flight?

They belong to all of us—
    these wild pets we share:
The graceful deer, the pesky raccoons,
    the red and blue birds everywhere.

Our paradise of wildlife
　　is a colorful garden too;
Evergreen trees and beautiful wildflowers
　　adorn our country zoo.

We are blessed to be a part
　　of this world God has made;
For the hustle and bustle of the city,
　　this life we would not trade.

Come on over neighbor,
　　the coffee is brewing;
The fruit cake is sweet,
　　and the garden vegetables are stewing.

Neighbor, we'd love for you to drop by,
　　you don't need a reason;
Just come on over
　　during this blessed Christmas season.

Come on over neighbor
　　and sit awhile;
We'd like to share some time with you;
　　we'd like to see your smile.

*I wrote this poem for a dear friend, Teresa Shivers, who shared the idea
for this poem.*

Leather Bound Friends

I think I will curl up and spend
    Some time today with an old friend.
I could learn about China of "yester-year"
    From Pearl Buck—a friend so dear.

Or perhaps I could learn about Adam's wife,
    Or some other historical life,
While I curl up alone
    With another author friend—Irving Stone.

James Herriot could tell me about
    Creatures great and small,
And how all things wise and wonderful
    The Lord God made them all.

Or, maybe C. S. Lewis has something to say
    That would cause me to be more reflective today.
Nature's beauty with Thoreau I could rehearse,
    Or share with Longfellow a special verse.

I could spend some time with the poet I love best,
    My dear friend, Edgar Guest.
Then, of course, there's David, Rebecca, and Paul,
    Friends from my favorite source of all.

With these friends, and more, it's hard to decide
    How and with whom my time I will divide.
But, it's sure nice to have time to spend
    With my many Leather Bound Friends.

Handshakes and Hugs

What a beautiful evening:
    "Meet the Teacher Night",
Hugs to new fourth graders,
    such a beautiful sight.

Granddaughter took pictures
    of the many new families;
We're starting a new journey
    to make special memories.

A favorite candy bar and diet coke
    was a special gift;
It will be sure to revive this teacher
    with a needed lift.

One mom commented she loved
    The Book on my desk;
"I love it too!"–of all my books,
    it is definitely the best.

Hugging former students
    brought much joy,
"Look, this tall young man
    was once my little boy!"

Handshakes of parents—
　　my partners this year,
Together we will teach
　　each boy and girl so dear.

To be a teacher—one
　　of life's greatest joys!
Thank you, Lord, for
　　all the girls and boys!

Father, to teach each student,
　　I will do my very best,
Thank You for handshakes
　　and hugs; I am so blessed.

*I was blessed to teach fourth grade at North Rock Creek Elementary
School in Shawnee, Oklahoma, for 32 years before I retired in 2020.*

To Be a Teacher

I was gathering what I needed for the day—
    I had planned a lot of things to do;
Sweet little Brooklyn grinned and said,
    "I want to be a teacher just like you!"

"Oh Brooklyn, that's a great idea;
    you will be the very best teacher of all."
I knew I wanted to be a teacher from
    the time I was very small.

I am so glad she wants to be a teacher.

Teaching is fun; I love those kids and
    no two days are ever the same;
After a day with 6th, 7th, and 8th graders,
    I happily headed to a ballgame.

I wanted to watch a basketball game,
    especially those senior boys;
Teaching those young athletes in fourth
    grade was one of my greatest joys.

I'm so glad I decided to be a teacher.

There at the Shawnee High School
    where the game was taking place,
I was given a hug by a handsome young
    man with a familiar face.

Ryan was my fourth grade student a few
        years ago and I was happy to hear
He graduated college and is teaching
        high school Social Studies this year.

I'm so happy he chose to be a teacher.

Thank you to all you hardworking friends
        who made this choice with me;
You know there are blessings unimaginable—
        blessings and challenges; it's not easy.

You chose to make a difference in the lives of
        students; your hard work is worth it all!
Thank you for caring for young people from
        the older students to the ones so small.

Thank you for deciding to be a teacher.

Sunshine in His Pocket

There was a boy –
    A boy who carried
        sunshine in his pocket...

He woke one morning
    as the sunbeams kissed his face;
He jumped out of bed
    and got dressed, as if in a race.
He found a wrinkled shirt
    on the floor,
And dirty socks over
    by the door.

He waved "bye" to his mom
    who was still in bed;
She wore a cloud of sadness
    over her head.
"I'm off to school!" he shouted
    as he shot off like a rocket;
And, as he ran out the door,
    sunbeams fell into his pocket.

His teacher greeted him with a hug
    and a smile on her face;
"Come on in!" She said, "Hurry up
    and find your place."
It was hard to sit at his desk;
    he had so much energy to burn,
But, his teacher was kind
    and made it so much fun to learn.

She taught him with patience
    and keen understanding;
Her ways were never harsh
    or too demanding.
She told him about places
    he would love to go;
And helped him learn many things
    he needed to know.

The years have passed
    and the boy is grown,
He has a good job
    and a family of his own.
His home is a happy place
    free from hatred and strife;
He has three neat kids
    and a wonderful wife.

His memories of his mom
    are really sad;
She's gone now—
    he never knew his dad.
But, he often smiles when
    he remembers that teacher—
The one that wore the locket,
    The one who loved the boy...
The boy who carried
    sunshine in his pocket.

North Rock Creek's Got Talent

NRC's got talent—it was
    an amazing sight to see;
There was a scene from "Grease"
    with a little blond "Sandy".
There's "John Travolta" and
    "Olivia Newton John"
      —could you tell?
Those two kiddos
    danced amazingly well.

There was a tap dancing act—
    a pretty girl in a dazzling costume;
A cute cheerleader with colorful
    pom poms entertained the room.
And, what about those three
    lassoing a steer?
They knew how to handle a rope—
    that was very clear.

"The Voice" can't hold a candle
    to the talent at NRC!
Each girl and boy that sang
    did their songs so beautifully.
Comedians, hula hoop acts, tumbling—
    each a special treat;
The rhythm of that jazz band—
    it just couldn't be beat.

Two fellas knew how to handle
    those basketballs—what fun!
Look out Harlem Globetrotters;
    here they come.
An original song about fishing—
    sure to be a favorite one;
Pretty neat how a dad on his guitar
    accompanied his son.

The audience cheered and applauded
    to show their delight.
The folks who picked the talent
    for this show sure did it right!
Dr. Smith and teachers wrapped the show up
    with a rendition of "This is Me".
Yep, "North Rock Creek's Got Talent",
    and it was an amazing sight to see!

North Rock Creek School Talent Show: May 7, 2018.

The School Nurse

"It takes a community to raise a child,"
    many people have said,
To nurture and teach them and make
    sure they are clothed and fed.

And it takes a lot of people
    to keep a school going,
To help the kids learn and stay
    healthy as they are growing.

It takes parents encouraging as
    they send them on their way;
It takes the teachers helping as
    the children learn and play.

It takes the cooks preparing food
    to put a smile on their face,
And the maintenance people
    working hard to repair the place.

It takes an office staff
    to keep the records complete;
And the principal and superintendent
    to keep everyone on their feet.

But the person the child needs when
    things are good or at their worst;
The person who fills a multitude of needs
    the child needs the school nurse!

She's there to make sure immunizations
    are up to date;
And to give breathing treatments when
    a child's asthma can't wait.

She's there for the six year old with a
    drawing of a heart on her hand,
"My blood sugar is 295; it's Valentine's Day;
    it's more than I can stand!"

The nurse is there with a rose and a little
    white bear so sweet;
"I know you can't have candy and cookies,
    but here's a special treat!"

She's there to do screenings: vision, hearing,
    scoliosis, and head lice too;
She's there to give hugs when a child is hurting
    or just feeling blue.

She's there for a headache, a skin rash, a bump,
    a bruise, a bloody nose;
She's there for a hang-nail, a broken arm, a
    black eye, or a stubbed toe.

She's there to give medications and to help
    take care of the staff.
She can take blood pressure, give a Tylenol,
    or just share a good laugh.

She's there to teach the importance
    of prevention:
Dental care, hygiene, drug awareness,
    and AIDS education.

She's there to be an extension of the Master's
    heart and hands;
And to hear Him say, "Well done," when
    before Him she stands.

Yes, it takes a community to raise a child;
    that is so very true.
In educating a child there is so much to
    teach and so much to do.

But, the person the child needs when
    things are good, or at their worst;
The person who fills a multitude
    of needs: The School Nurse.

I wrote this in 1997, for a wonderful school Nurse, Sheila Jordan, who helped take care of students and staff for several years at North Rock Creek School.

Dedicated to school nurses everywhere.

The Sunrise Over Lena's Place

In the early morning hours when the house
    is quiet, I have a lot of time to think.
Most mornings I start my day in the kitchen
    rinsing dishes at the kitchen sink.

There is a window above the sink where
    I watch the appearing of a new day;
I smile as I observe the crows eating last night's
    scraps and the feisty squirrels play.

This morning I thanked my Savior for the
    hope we have in His Amazing Grace—
A reminder that came to me from the
    beautiful sunrise over Lena's place.

Lena was my childhood friend from our
    little country school a long time ago;
Lena and I attended the same church
    where her grandchildren I came to know.

Lena was my neighbor across the field
    behind a stand of trees.
Lena—sometimes I would give her a phone
    call and sometimes she would call me.

Lena and I talked recently from her hospital
    room where she had a very long stay.
She missed her husband and grandchildren
    and was to be dismissed just any day.

We don't always understand why
    things happen the way they do;
But, our precious Savior said, "Child, come
    home, your work on Earth is through."

Lena is in Heaven now, completely healed,
    and celebrating His Amazing Grace—
A reminder that came to me from the
    beautiful sunrise over Lena's place.

Somewhere Right Now

Somewhere right now a warm glow surrounds
    a family because of a wedding's success,
And a warm glow of happiness surrounds Mayweather,
    though I bet his face is a mess.

Somewhere right now an elderly couple are fearing
    the rise of water that has covered their floor,
And across the world elderly grandparents wonder
    if they will have fresh drinking water anymore.

Somewhere right now people are reaching out—
    giving all they have to bring relief,
While somewhere down a flooded street, a fellow
    is armed—ready to shoot a thief.

Somewhere a pastor is up early putting finishing
    touches on his sermon notes;
Praying he can bring hope to folks who have left
    flooded homes by rescue boats.

Somewhere right now there is laughter and tears,
    and there is joy—in spite of sorrow;
And somewhere there is the strength to know
    there will be courage for tomorrow.

Somewhere there is a poet mulling this
    all over in her head,
Thoughts tumbling down on paper while
    others are still in bed.

Thinking about the "somewheres" and the
    "someones" from Houston to Macau,
Praying for each of you to have needed strength
    and courage somewhere right now.

Floyd Mayweather Jr. defeated Conor McGregor in the 10th round on August 26, 2017, at the T-Mobile Arena in Paradise, Nevada.

Hurricane Harvey made landfall in Houston, Texas, on August 25, 2017. The Category 4 hurricane took 36 lives and flooded at least 134,170 homes.

Typhoon Hato struck the coast of China, August 23, 2017, bringing massive winds and flooding to the Cities of Macau and Hong Kong. At least 12 people died as a result of the typhoon.

I Shouldn't Have Read That Thread

Restless night—couldn't sleep;
    tossed and turned on my bed.
I knew what was going on:
    I shouldn't have read that thread!

Political parties at war with ideas,
    each accusing the other of insanity,
While the voice of reason tries to remind us
    of the kindness of humanity.

A thought typed in good will,
    words written in a simple post,
Ignites anger in some; just something
    to think about by most.

Too much to think about late at night—
    conflicting thoughts in my head.
I would have slept so much better
    if I just hadn't read that thread!

"A microchip in your hand
    if you're going to work here,"
This statement sparked heated
    words and ignited fear.

"The Bible says it's *The Mark*,"
    one person tries to explain;
"The Bible is just a bunch of nonsense."
    (This statement causes pain.)

"Zeus save us!" one person
    comments in jest.
"Who is Jesus (Hey-sous)?
    He mows my lawn the best!"

Words spoken harshly
    and carelessly from the start;
Some show no respect
    for the sacred things of the heart.

The idea of a chip
    fills my heart with dread,
And I tell myself,
    "I shouldn›t have read that thread!"

Ideas are exchanged—have been
    since the beginning of time;
Free dialogue, free press—to forbid
    this practice is a crime.

I like the sharing of ideas;
    we learn and grow that way.
Even when I don't agree, I want
    to know what you have to say.

But, from now on, at bedtime,
    I'm clearing all conflict from my head,
So when the sun comes up, I won't have to say,
    "I shouldn't have read that thread!"

A Poem for a Friend
(Thirty Years in the Making)

With quiet tenderness she taught her classes
    with determination and love.
Teaching was not a job, but a calling on
    her life from above.

She loved her students enough to guide them
    with high expectations.
If you were a student of Mrs. Bell's, there
    would be some basic realizations.

You would know you would write "in cursive"
    the minute you walked in the door.
You were taught to be respectful and responsible,
    and so much more.

You sang "The Star Spangled Banner," said "Please,"
    "Thank you," and "Yes Ma'am".
Doors were to be closed quietly and lockers
    you should never slam.

She came early—often
    the first teacher to arrive.
She stayed late, working hard to help
    each of her students thrive.

She was so prepared and organized;
    I was always amazed.
If she was ever frustrated,
    her voice she never raised.

Her teacher's guides and supplies
    were always in place.
(She did misplace a student teacher once—
    you should have seen her face!)

Mrs. Bell's fourth grade classroom was
    a positive and pretty place to be:
Motivational sayings, student's work
    displayed, and pictures of her family.

I have watched her family grow over the years
    as grandchildren have come along.
I have witnessed my friend say, "Good-bye" to loved
    ones, and with God's help stay strong.

What a joy, a blessing, and
    a privilege to call her friend;
She inspired me to be a better teacher
    until my NRC years came to an end.

We studied together, traveled together, and laughed
    together so much through the years;
We have prayed together and helped each other
    through times of sorrow and tears.

We studied Native American Languages three
    summers in a row;
We made presentations in Washington D. C. and
    Hawaii–wonderful places to go.

We were determined to find a black sand beach
    in Hawaii–who would have supposed?
We laughed at ourselves when we realized the beach
    guests' birthday suits were completely exposed.

We collaborated with many team members,
    planning lessons for fourth grade.
When you work so closely with colleagues,
    many friendships are made.

Mrs. Esther Bell has served as secretary, treasurer,
  vice-president, and president of P.O.E.
A blessing to the Professional Oklahoma Educators,
  I know you would all agree.

She has served in many leadership positions and
  has been a professional in every way;
What a joy to be able to celebrate her many years
  at North Rock Creek on this special day.

We know this new chapter in her life will find her
  busy serving others—that's what she does best.
Time with family and friends, time to read,
  maybe even time to rest.

She has made a difference in so many lives
  teaching with determination and love.
Teaching was not just a job, but a calling
  on her life from above.

*I wrote this poem for my dear friend, Esther Bell, and read it at her
retirement reception on October 28, 2021. Mrs. Bell and I taught
fourth grade together for nearly 30 years. My life has truly been enriched
from our wonderful friendship.*

Fun

The Wonder of Words

Do you know just how
    much fun words can be?
Over the years words
    have been a treasure to me.
I love to write poems
    and words are my tools,
So are paper and pens
    and grammar rules.

With words you can travel
    to many a destination;
You can walk, or run, or fly;
    it's up to your imagination.
Here's an interesting fact:
    the more words you know,
In your imagination,
    the more places you can go.

Have fun with words; read them,
    write them, illustrate them too.
Share the beauty of words with others;
    it's all up to you.
Yes, words can be wonderful;
    they've been a treasure to me;
Do you, my dear friends, know
    just how magical words can be?

Ode to the Toothbrush

You're a useful little tool
    I've been told by people galore;
I have bought so many of you
    at the Walmart store.

I've chided my boys to use you:
    brush, brush, rinse, and spit.
I've bought thousands of you;
    there's no doubt about it!

In our bathroom, so many of you
    have been hanging around;
You have played music as your bristles
    danced up and down.

You have lit up with a timer
    that runs for a minute;
All kinds of clever holders
    have held you in it!

What did the moms do
    when cavemen roamed free?
Did they make their kids
    chew bark from a nearby tree?

I wonder how moms got kids
    to brush in covered wagon days.
I wish I knew how to get my kids
    to use you; what are the ways?

I've pleaded and scolded and
	put you in each boy's hand.
I've given rewards and consequences;
	I just don't understand!

You just sit there all smug;
	you don't do your work.
I can just see your unused bristles
	give me a smirk!

So, though I am rarely a quitter,
	I just give up!
You can idly rest there
	in each boy's little cup.

If their teeth rot and and fall out
	by the time they are 29,
They better not come to me;
	I will not listen to them whine!

I've done everything I can imagine
	for nine long years;
I'm puttin' a smile on my face
	and I'm wipin' my tears!

I'm giving the job to you,
	Toothbrush, and them alone!
Hmm, wonder if there is a way
	to put bristles on a cell phone?

The Evolution of Fried Chicken

When I was just a little girl I watched my
    Grandma Souders make fried chicken;
It was quite a process but those crunchy tender
    chicken pieces were finger licken.

She had a bunch of chickens in her backyard
    where I would run and play;
Those happy free ranging chickens never knew
    when it would be their last day!

My little grandma would come out that back
    door with a determined look on her face;
Those chickens would be cluckin' and squawkin'
    and runnin' all over the place.

Grandma would quickly grab one of those ole
    fat hens and quickly wring its neck;
I wonder if the rest of the brood huddled
    together and whispered, "Oh heck!"

I'd help her pluck the feathers and watch her
    carefully clean that ole hen;
She'd skillfully cut it into pieces, roll it in flour,
    and put it in a sizzlin' hot pan.

She'd make some biscuits from scratch and
    stir up an iron skillet of gravy;
I didn't know it then but those were some
    good cooking lessons she gave me.

Now, fast forward a few years, and how
    I loved watching my mama cook!
She loved feeding her family and we were
    so joyful when she made us a recipe book.

My mama could take a frozen hen from the
    freezer and before you knew it
She had that chicken thawed, cut up, rolled
    in flour, and sizzlin' in a skillet.

A few years on down the road and I'm the
    mama in the kitchen feeding my family;
I never raised chickens but fried chicken
    dinners, I've served up plenty.

I prefer to buy those chicken tenders all
    cut up and ready to go;
Roll 'em in flour, salt and pepper, brown
    'em in hot oil and cook 'em slow.

Them finger licken fried chicken dinners
    keep changing from when I was small;
You can pick 'em up at a "drive through" or
    have KFC deliver by Uber drivers y'all!

There's even something called "plant based
    chicken"—there's no chicken in it;
I saw that on a KFC ad and just imagined
    Colonel Sanders saying, "Wait a minute!"

Chicken dinners have changed a lot since
    I was a child watching Grandma cook,
But, the important things will never
    change—the words written in the Book.

God's promises are rock solid and on His
    Truth you can forever take a stand;
No matter how the world changes, we'll
    be secure as long as we cling to His hand.

I am not an evolutionist because I believe
    every word in the Bible is true;
But, I do believe those fried chicken dinners
    have evolved, my friend, don't you?

Sasquatch

There, lurking in some trees, just
    off River Road a little way,
Stalks a figure that's a little foreboding,
    I would have to say!

He's a creepy being about 8 foot tall
    and he's brown and hairy.
If you should happen upon him late
    at night, it would be very scary!

He walks on tippy toes with his strong
    back kind of bent.
Some say he isn't real, but we know he is;
    we will not relent!

There, where the goats play and a camel
    lives, you better watch!
He's there and he's real; we know 'cause
    we saw him: Sasquatch!

Me and the Panic Button

I've got a friend from which I
   would never want to part,
Especially when I'm making a trip
   to the friendly Walmart.

It seems, at times, my shopping
   trip takes a long time to end,
Especially if I have stopped to
   chat with a dear friend.

I love shopping at Walmart—
   most of my friends know;
My family needs many things and the
   cart gets harder to push as I go.

By the time I've made it to the check-out,
   another basket is usually needed;
When the checker asks if I need help,
   the suggestion is rarely heeded.

With determination and two baskets
   of treasures, to the car I embark;
Too often I realize, with a dreadful
   feeling, "Where did I park?"

Just when I think I'm going to
   have to call Willie to rescue me,
I remember I have a dear friend,
   there in my hand, on my car key!

Hoping the noise doesn't startle any
   bystanders standing around,
I press that magic button and listen
   for that wonderful honking sound.

Sure enough, I hear it… there it is!
    At the sound, my heart is elated.
The person who invented that Panic
    Button could never be overrated.

I tell myself, "Next time I will pay
    attention where I park my car."
I've heard it's a really good thing to
    know where you are.

But, I probably won't; so, me and the
    Panic Button will never part,
Especially when I make my weekly
    trip to the friendly Walmart.

Counting Sheep

It was the middle of the night
    and I just couldn't sleep,
So, I decided I would try counting
    the proverbial sheep.

In my mind I created a field
    of wildflowers and clover,
And a white picket fence the fluffy
    critters could jump over.

A pretty ewe gracefully cleared
    that fence with a leap,
And started bleating encouragement
    to the other sheep.

The oldest lamb started to follow
    after his mother,
But was pushed out of the way
    by his ornery little brother.

The whole flock stopped grazing
    in my imagined field,
Watching to see if the determined
    big brother would yield.

He didn't, of course; he knew
    it was his job to lead the way;
So he bleated to his brother,
    "Wait your turn and do what I say!"

The little guy leaped the fence
    without listening to his brother,
And all the other sheep started
    pushing and shoving each other.

Well, the whole counting sheep
    ended because chaos ensued,
As some of the flock started
    acting down right rude!

I know this is not the way
    this is supposed to go…
But, I just can't keep my sheep
    jumping in a row.

So I left that pretty field
    of wildflowers and clover,
The attempt to get sleepy
    by counting sheep was over!

I'll just get up and read
    my Bible and pray.
I'll be just fine;
    who needs sleep anyway?

Where Fairies Dance

There, near the old tree stump
    underneath the blue sky,
You may just see some silky wings
    go fluttering by.

You may just spot a pretty fairy mommy
    grasping wee little hands,
As the winged creatures dance
    to the chirping of the cricket bands!

Tiny little beings, sometimes so small
    you can barely see,
Ride across puddles on little leaves
    as they travel leisurely.

Little creatures may hitch a ride
    when Mr. Cricket comes along,
If the little tuxedoed fellow is not
    too tired from his chirping song.

Mushrooms are the perfect place
    to join the elves for a picnic,
Using tiny little forks and spoons
    crafted from a weathered stick.

Tiny acorns filled with fresh rainwater
    make the nicest little drinking cups,
With a drop of nectar for flavor
    from the pretty primrose buttercups.

Elves build tiny houses out of tree stumps
    with bold determination,
And fairies dance and giggle in the carefree
    world of a child's imagination.

The Play House

There is no sight more beautiful
    on any given day
Than the precious vision of
    little children at play.

In this house we are often
    blessed with this scene,
Which makes it kind of hard
    to keep the house clean.

Now, I think I will get some order
    in these many toys
That are often strung out by
    little girls and boys.

"I have a wonderful idea,"
    I think to myself,
"I'll choose one room and
    put the toys on a shelf."

The kids can keep the toys
    in that room when they come,
We'll have less clutter in this house–
    well, at least some.

The den's a big room, it will
    be perfect, I decide;
On a shelf behind the couch
    the Lincoln Logs I hide.

Maybe the dining room would
    be a better place–
These games in the closet will
    bring a smile to their face.

On second thought, the kitchen
   is just right for Play-Doh,
And this is a perfect place to keep the
   water paints—this I know!

Then again, the bathroom needs
   some tiny boats and toy dishes,
So a little one can sail a boat or play
   in the water if he or she wishes.

Now my bedroom is really not
   the perfect place to play,
But, I'll keep just a few "dress-up"
   things in there anyway.

One room—the one with the entry door—
   we will keep it clean;
But, to move those big ole stuffed horses—
   that would be mean.

The extra bedrooms—the little one
   and the bigger one too,
That's where we will keep the
   cars and the floating toy zoo.

I guess each room's the playroom;
   that just leaves the hall—
A perfect place to put our children's
   pictures on the wall.

Toys in every room and I guess
   that's the way it will stay,
So every room can be filled with
   the joy of children at play.

It may not look like a magazine house—
   a little cluttered it may be;
But, it is the perfect house—the perfect
   playhouse—at least to me.

Mama Danced A Jig in the Kitchen

That was about the funniest thing
    I have ever seen;
I hope that doesn't sound ornery
    or downright mean,
'Cause Mama laughed too, but
    not right away, I might mention,
That Saturday morning when Mama
    danced a jig in the kitchen.

Mama's serious about cooking, but
    with such joy on her face;
She loves to chop, measure, stir—the
    kitchen is her happy place.
So, I couldn't help but wonder what
    on earth was going on,
When I heard screamin' replace Mama's
    usual "Happy Place" song.

She was stompin' and wavin' and yellin'
    something about gettin' a cat.
"Mama, what's got into you?" I laughed,
    "Why are you actin' like that?"
"Well," she remarked, getting her composure
    as she ran out the kitchen door,
"That gave me the heebie jeebies; a mouse
    just ran across the floor!"

Bravely back to her cooking she went
    with a concerned look on her face.
No silly mouse was going to keep Mama
    from her "Happy Place".
But, that sure gave us a good laugh and
    grabbed our attention,
The Saturday mornin' when Mama
    danced a jig in the kitchen!

The Monopoly Money

I'm blessed to live in the house where I grew up,
    and sometimes my memories are funny.
One of the silliest I want to share is the one of
    we kids and our Monopoly money.
Now, we used that money the way it was intended
    and played games on end.
Usually it was just my brothers and me—sometimes
    we were joined by a friend.

We played in the woods, at an old booth from the
    restaurant of an auntie dear,
But, our favorite place was at the kitchen table;
    that memory is very clear.
Sometimes an upset sibling would push the board
    off the table and the money would fly!
Our mother did her best to teach us to be good
    sports; she really did try!

One cold rainy day Mother let us take all the cans
    out of the cabinet and play store.
That's one way we used that Monopoly money,
    but I could tell you about more.
You've heard of "Dirty Money"; well, ours got
    extremely dirty from our grimy hands.
So we washed and ironed all that money—
    wonder who came up with that funny plan.

I value my mind's treasures of growing up in
    This house—many memories so funny.
With, of course, one of the best: we kids and
    our Monopoly money.

The Nickel Lemon

I'd like to share a memory—just one,
    though there are many more,
Of a reading lesson, a nickel, a lemon,
    and a little country store.

Our teacher, Mrs. Cheek, taught children
    how to read—including me,
At a little round table, from *Alice and Jerry*
    in a reading group of three.

We read those fun stories as we learned
    the magic of the written word;
Mrs. Cheek smiled—no telling how many
    times the stories she had heard!

The day would finally come,
    after a week or two,
When we had read the little book
    all the way through.

If we children could read the list of
    new words at the end of the book,
Mrs. Cheek would give us a nickel and
    we would give her a joyful look.

That was so exciting to hold that nickel
    and feel such pride, but there's more,
We "rich" little children would take that nickel
    and, during recess, walk to the store.

Just a little way to the little country store
    we would walk through the sand,
Skipping and giggling, carefully grasping
    the treasured coin in our hand.

The sound of a little bell greeted us
    when we opened the door,
Mr. Franklin was waiting behind
    the counter of the little store.

We could have bought a candy bar, five
    penny candies, or a pack of gum,
But a bright yellow lemon was our choice—
    eating it would be so much fun!

We hurriedly skipped back to school and
    asked the cook to cut our lemon in half;
Mrs. Harp did just as we asked and gave
    it back to us with a cheerful laugh.

We rushed out to the playground
    where the boys were running races;
We slurped on those sour lemons just
    to see the funny looks on their faces.

Oh, those were simpler times and
    I treasure the memories galore,
One of my favorites will always be a nickel,
    a lemon, and a little country store.

This memory is from about the years 1956 or '57 when I was in first or second grade. Mrs. Cheek taught grades 1-4 in one room of the two room school while Mr. Cheek taught 5-8. They lived across the road in the "teacherage".

The Fish Feast

Willie cleaned the freezer out to make room
    for good ole venison meat;
Garrison's success at hunting on our "North Forty"
    led to this special treat.

The little freezer in the cellar shed hadn't been
    cleaned out in way too long;
And, even though it was outdated, throwing out
    freezer-burned fish just seemed wrong.

But the story Willie shared with me about
    the "fish feast" enjoyed by hungry birds,
Made the discard of the ole fish worthwhile;
    I loved hearing his entertaining words.

Seems two hawks found the frozen delicacy
    and began to happily eat;
Along came a shiny black crow hungrily
    eyeing the special fish treat.

The hawks were not concerned about the crow—
    didn't offer to share at all;
And the poor ole crow wasn't about to invite
    himself through the invisible wall.

So the hawks—twice the size of the crow—
    kept pullin' off the frozen chunks of meat,
While the little lone crow hopped this way and
    that way longing for a bite to eat.

He turned his head from side to side
    and did his little crow dance;
Oh, how he wished those selfish hawks
    would just give him a chance.

Willie had to leave after a while and
    couldn't stay for the entire dinner show;
I sure hope those hawks got full and
    saved a little for that determined crow.

Onomatopoeia

Onomatopoeia is such
  a fun word to say;
It's sure not a word
  you hear every day.

The bacon is *sizzling*;
  someone *slammed* the door.
The clock goes *tick tick*; someone's shoes
  go *clip clop* on the floor.

"*Waaa*," goes the baby;
  the cat keeps saying, "*Meow*."
If I needed quiet to explain this word,
  I wouldn't know how.

The pesky fly keeps *buzzing*
  around my head,
While my sweet husband
  snores softly in bed.

There's a dog going *woof* outside and someone's
  tires are *screeching* on the road;
The washing machine is making a funny *ernk*
  ernk ernk with too big a load.

I just wanted to explain this word but it's too
  noisy to think!
There's an aggravating *drip, drip, drip* coming
  from the kitchen sink.

Wham! Slam! Boom! Bang!
  There are sounds all around,
And the clue to the meaning
  of onomatopoeia can be found.

Yep, it's not a word
  you hear every day,
But onomatopoeia
  is a fun word to say!

How to Eat a Watermelon

Watermelon can be eaten
 in many kind of ways;
I like to eat 'em like people
 did in the "olden days"!

Not sittin' at a table with a fork
 and a nap-kin,
But outside, with sweet red juice
 drippin' from my chin!

First you take hold of the fruit with
 two hands—a thin slice is nice;
Then you say a kind "thank you" to
 the person who gave you the slice.

You gotta lean over just a little
 before you take a bite;
The juice will go on the ground,
 not your shoes, if you do it right.

Now about those seeds—what in the world
 will you do with 'em?
It's really kinda simple—don't let them
 become a big prob-lem!

You can pick them out one at a time
 And gently toss them down,
Or you can take a bite with them,
 And spit 'em on the ground.

Now when you finish that sweet juicy fruit,
 please don't eat that rind.
Find a trash can and throw that part away;
 that would be really kind.

Now go somewhere and rinse your fingers;
    they're probably pretty sticky.
You may even need to rinse your face
    if it's all sweet and icky!

Yes, watermelon can be eaten
    in many ways;
But this is how it was done
    in the olden' days!

Much more fun than usin'
    a fork and a nap-kin,
Outside, with sweet, red juice
    drippin' from your chin!

At the beginning of many school years, my hardworking husband would deliver 20-25 huge watermelons he had grown to share with students and staff at North Rock Creek School.

The counter of my fourth grade classroom would be full of watermelons. With the help of teacher friends, we served juicy red, ripe slices to about three hundred students from pre-k through fifth grade.

One year, a dear friend, the school librarian, Bonne Hutton, took pictures of the children as they enjoyed the watermelon slices on the grassy areas of the school grounds and created a colorful book with the photos and this poem. What treasured memories!

I'm So Glad

There was a kind of funky smell this morning
    when I opened my bedroom door.
It was quite a bit later when I found the source
    covered up on the living room floor.
I'm so glad…

Glad I had ventured into the backyard to drink
    in the beauty of a new day;
Glad I had ventured back in time to sing "Onward
    Christian Soldiers," with Brother Ray.
I'm so glad…

Glad I had opened the Book and gained needed
    wisdom from the word.
Glad my soul was singing–joyfully cherishing
    the Gospel message I've heard.
I'm so glad…

Glad I had an hour or so to wake up with a
    cup of coffee–maybe more,
When I discovered the towel hiding something
    on the living room floor.
I'm so glad…

Glad I had the resources, the strength, and the
    time to clean up that mess,
Glad my heart was so full of His joy; it just
    didn't cause me any stress.
I'm so glad..

Glad my daddy taught me, "Don't sweat the
    small stuff," and this was no big deal!
Someone in this house knows what I cleaned
    up, but they're sleeping still.
And it's OK…and, I'm so glad!

A Thinner Me

"Dress to look thinner,"
    the magazine article said,
So I determined to do that
    when I hopped out of bed.

I put on my "ten pound slimmer"
    control-top hose;
The slimming black outfit from
    my closet I chose.

Next, I remembered to choose
    great big earrings.
(I'll look five pounds thinner
    by choosing these things.)

That's fifteen pounds I have lost
    without even trying.
More fun than going on a diet;
    there's no denying!

Now for the makeup; put it
    on carefully–don't rush!
Bring out those cheekbones
    with a little dark blush.

Now I put on the black pumps,
    the ones that pinches;
They hurt my feet, but I need
    those slimming inches.

Next, I worked on the hair;
    I needed a really big "do".
That was in the article titled
    "How to be a Slimmer You."

I tried a few other tricks
    that were supposed to melt fat;
I looked in the mirror and
    thought "Wow, who is that?"

The person smiling back at me
    was almost too thin;
"Better eat a stack of pancakes,"
    I thought with a grin!

Should I Write Another Poem?

"Should I write another poem?"
    I asked my sweet Willie.
"Your brain should be drained," he replied.
    (That is just silly!)

Words dance in my head
    about when our kids were small;
My brain is so full of poems,
    I could never write them all.

There's the beauty of nature:
    blue and green and sunshiny bright.
There are breathtaking clouds,
    bright stars, and the moon at night.

There are friends to write about
    and cherished memories to share.
There are so many stories to put into verse;
    stories are everywhere!

The paper is my palette; the pen my brush—
    to paint with words, I must!
These poems will bring a smile, some comfort,
    or a little bit of joy, I trust.

No, my brain is not drained,
    sweet husband of mine;
There's always another poem to write,
    if I could just find the time.

CPSIA information can be obtained
at www.ICGtesting.com
Printed in the USA
BVHW042045200223
658864BV00002B/21